# Honey,
# I Homeschooled
# the Kids

# Honey, I Homeschooled the Kids

### Nadia Sawalha
### and
### Mark Adderley

CORONET

First published in Great Britain in 2020 by Coronet
An Imprint of Hodder & Stoughton
An Hachette UK company

This paperback edition published in 2021

1

A CIP catalogue record for this title
is available from the British Library

Paperback ISBN 9781529351354
eBook ISBN 9781529350609

Typeset in ITC Mendoza by
Palimpsest Book Production Ltd, Falkirk, Stirlingshire

Printed and bound in Great Britain by Clays Ltd, Elcograf S.p.A.

Hodder & Stoughton policy is to use papers that are natural,
renewable and recyclable products and made from wood grown in
sustainable forests. The logging and manufacturing processes are expected
to conform to the environmental regulations of the country of origin.

Hodder & Stoughton Ltd
Carmelite House
50 Victoria Embankment
London EC4Y 0DZ

www.hodder.co.uk

'Only connect'
E. M. Forster, *Howards End*


'War was easier than daughters'
*Game of Thrones*

For our precious girls Maddie and Kiki.
THANK YOU for your patience.
We are, after all, just adult kids ourselves and,
as Finn (from *Adventure Time*) once said,
"Everything small is just a smaller
version of something big!"

# Contents

# Introduction

Before we start, we'd like to ask *you* a question and present *you* with a challenge. Sit back or, if you're standing in a bookshop reading these first few paragraphs, stay standing exactly where you are. Now, close your eyes and clear your mind. Next, try to slowly visualise the quintessential image of a homeschooled child.

Really take your time. Flesh out the picture. What are they wearing? How do they look? What's their demeanour? How do they interact? What sort of parents do they have? Indeed, *do* they have parents?! See them in your mind's eye and don't shy away from cliché or stereotype.

If you're struggling here are a few suggestions:

Does he or she wear scruffy baggy clothes? Do they look pale and wan? Is veganism or vegetarianism their likely diet? Do they have butterflies sewn onto their dungarees? Do they look like a young Bob Dylan? Do they have head lice? Are they barefoot, running through the woods, crafting bows and arrows out of cedar wood? Are their parents Extinction Rebellion activists? Is their sport of choice skateboarding?

Or does your image sit at the opposite end of the spectrum? Well-behaved, quiet, obedient children, with shiny plaited hair; strict and overbearing religious zealots for parents? Potential victims of radicalisation or sectarianism due to issues around faith, lifestyle or a rejection of mainstream morals?

Or perhaps you're seeing those kids that are referred to in the press as 'school refusers' or 'system crashers'; those who cannot be tolerated for behavioural reasons, whose parents are themselves delinquents, and who are falling through the social care system?

Perhaps you don't even think of the child at all? Maybe your image is of lazy parents, who don't want to conform because they can't be arsed, who take benign neglect to the next level (verging on abuse), parents who never grew up . . . 'vandals in sandals' as Mark calls them or happy-clappies as Nadia calls them?

Finally, of course, there's another category of kid who for very valid learning-difficulty reasons *has* to be taught outside the conventional schooling system.

Did your image fall into any of these camps? Honestly? Don't be afraid if it did. Perhaps your image was even more extreme? Maybe they were smoking spliffs or were young entrepreneurs running a microbrewery at the age of eight?

Either way, we won't be offended, and we certainly wouldn't be surprised.

You see, back in 2015, when we first took our youngest daughter Kiki-Bee out of school, we too had an image of homeschooled children that featured virtually every one of these stereotypes and clichés; some too rude to print. At its simplest, back then, homeschooling was for people or families who lived their lives (out of choice or necessity) very much outside the mainstream system. It was for people who had turned their backs on convention; anarchists, radicals, hippies, eccentrics, ideologues. It certainly wasn't something for *us*! If you'd said then that we would have both gone on to homeschool our kids we'd have spat our oat milk cappuccinos across the room! Homeschooling?! Us?! No way! We weren't homeschoolers!

How wrong could we have been?

*March 2020 – The week lockdown was announced and most of the UK's school children were told to stay at home.*

*Nadia: Kiki. Kiki. Wake up.*
*Kiki: GROANS*

*Nadia: Kiki . . . Guess what?!*
*Kiki: Whaaaatttt?*
*Nadia: The whole world is now being*
*   homeschooled.*
*Kiki: WHHHHATTTTTTT??!?!*

*Maddie: Dad! Dad!*
*Mark: Morning sweetie. You okay?*
*Maddie: Dad!!*
*Mark: What?!?!*
*Maddie: They're calling the way we live*
*   'Quarantine'!*

Homeschooling our girls was *never* an easy choice. It wasn't an ideological choice. We often say, 'We never went in search of homeschooling; homeschooling very much found us!' It's strange to think that some *six* years later, something we had no knowledge of, something we considered a bit crackpot and weird, has become our 'new normal'.

Right now, as we write, parents all over the world have been introduced to the concept of homeschooling their kids in a very sudden and brutal fashion. Choice has been removed. The U word is being bandied around everywhere. With schools closed, parents have been left (in lockdown) sitting across from their children facing the prospect of being mum, dad and now . . . teacher! It is, as they say . . . UNPRECEDENTED!

In many ways, this sudden change of circumstances – the rapidity with which lockdown was enforced and the speed with which parents were thrust into a teaching and learning maelstrom – echoes the way in which we too fell into homeschooling back in 2015. Although for the vast majority of parents who homeschool their kids in normal day-to-day life it is a choice, choice wasn't really part of the equation when we decided to pull Kiki-Bee out of school. We can therefore empathise with the palpable shock of suddenly finding yourself almost entirely responsible for your kids' education . . . sat at your kitchen table . . . or on your sofa . . . wondering if the Wi-Fi is going to be strong enough.

Our hearts have really gone out to parents the length and breadth of the country who found themselves suddenly at sea trying to safeguard and protect their children's learning, with nothing other than the at times limited online help of their schools.

That's why we felt there was perhaps no better time than now to share our experiences (the good and the bad) as we too tried to navigate our ways through the choppy waters of a strange new world!

However, our desire to write about our experiences now isn't just about the parallels we encountered at the point we turned our backs on conventional schooling. We also want to help alleviate some of the fear, worry and anxiety that necessarily comes with being responsible for your children's education and learning. Having witnessed so many parents tearing their hair out and fretting about hitting this or that academic threshold or target in the school environment – there have been countless occasions when we've wanted to reach out or shout out: 'STOP!!! Don't go so fast! Stop beating yourselves up! Don't make the same mistakes we made!!! There's no need to RUSH at this!' (We must stress, that while we will be using the term 'parent' throughout this book, we will be using it in the broadest sense of the word, in order to encompass *all* shades of parenthood, whether it be grandparents, carers, step-parents, siblings or guardians.)

For us, the Covid-19 crisis has in one way presented parents with the obvious difficulty of trying to home-school their kids but, if looked at differently, it also throws up countless opportunities for change, adjustment and a different type of learning. Bizarrely, this crisis offers all parents an opportunity to reconsider the very concept of schooling and learning. It may sound a bit hippy to say this, but the global pandemic has given us the chance to see things differently: the way we work, the way we travel, the way we consume, the way we use the planet and (of course) the way we learn *and* the way we teach our children.

It's important to say from the outset that just because we have homeschooled both our girls now for the past six years, we have never been *anti*-school. For the vast majority of people, the schooling system (private or state) is entirely appropriate and correct. Many children do indeed find the *right* school. One that does what it says on the tin. But a huge number of kids find themselves in the wrong types of schools, trying to survive in a system that just doesn't serve them well, and for many, many parents and children, this one-size-fits-all approach to learning and teaching children isn't necessarily the right one. We simply believe that if you want to pursue an alternative approach to your child's education it shouldn't be stigmatised.

In sharing our story, we are not trying to persuade parents to take their kids out of school. Homeschooling isn't easy. There are many practical difficulties involved with it. It doesn't necessarily fit in with the ways many people and families live their lives. However, what we do want to achieve by writing this book is to address the prejudices, reiterate how achievable it is (if you can adjust your lives to accommodate it), but also (and perhaps most importantly) prove that there are *many, many* important strategies and techniques we've stumbled upon and discovered during our homeschooling journey that could prove enormously useful and beneficial to parents and children who have no intention whatsoever of turning their backs on school, but would like to cherry-pick some of the best bits of what homeschooling or, as we sometimes call it, 'Complementary Learning', can (at its best) offer up.

## Myth-busting

It is firmly our belief that the reason more people haven't chosen to homeschool is because it is still (despite its increasing popularity) shrouded in so much mystery, fear, judgement and fake news.

Why is *our* story a good one to share? Our journey hasn't been a smooth one, but then, if you think about it, *most* children's journeys through education aren't smooth ones. There are *always* hiccups en route. However, it has been our experience that in among the ranks of most parents there is a conspiracy of silence that seeks to deny, shield and cover-up any imperfections in our children's educations.

The peer pressure surrounding being a perfect parent in 2020, pretending that the system is working well for our kids, is probably more intense now than it has ever been in the history of parenting. But equally, this public image of parental perfection isn't *just* the preserve of parents with children in schools, it can be the preserve of homeschoolers too.

It seems that, regardless of how your kids are learning or, more importantly, how they are feeling, parents *always* need to be the *perfect* advocates or defendants of whatever educational system their kids find themselves in. If our children go to a grammar we will extol the virtues of grammar schools; boarding schools 'never did me any harm'; the state system 'is the real world in microcosm' . . . as parents we must *always* give an entirely positive spin on whatever system our kids find themselves in.

We have never claimed to be anything other than a couple of parents struggling to make sense of everything. Every decision we have made as parents has been made imperfectly, and so, in our advocacy of shaking up the ways in which we all view education, the last thing we are going to suggest in this book is the 'perfect' way to homeschool your child. We are anything *but* the perfect example of homeschoolers. Being parents, for us, has been a prolonged process of accepting our fallibilities, admitting our faults, embracing our mistakes, saying we're wrong when we are wrong, identifying our defects and letting go of the idea that we have the absolute solution to everything in our children's lives. We don't, we never have. We are just two grown-up children who happen to be parents – and sometimes admitting as much is the first step to some sort of freedom!

In a weird way, it's probably fair to say we often feel as though we sit as outside the homeschooling community as we do outside the conventional schooling community. Just as highly academic schools and high-achieving students can intimidate the smartest child (and their parents), so too are there many home-schooling parents and children who can seem incredibly intimidating, and who appear to be living an idyllic homeschooling life that the vast majority of us could only ever dream of replicating.

We therefore thought it would be best to share our thoughts and experiences in the form of both a shared voice and, at times, a split conversation; moving back and forth between the two of us. Although the journey has been a shared one, our perspectives on it have often been different and we haven't always agreed on the best way forward. The experiences of a father are different to those of a mother, and both of us – when we originally set out on this homeschooling journey – had completely different experiences and ideas about learning and education; we had totally different fears and hopes; and yet neither of us could have done it without the other. In those early days in the homeschooling wilderness, we craved, in our different ways, an approachable, informative, honest and non-judgemental guidebook to, or account of, the many pitfalls and joys of homeschooling, and that's what we have tried to create here.

Whenever Nadia has spoken about homeschooling on *Loose Women*, or whenever the two of us have both talked about the topic on our social media platforms, the interest has always spiked off the chart. There is a hunger to know what it's really like, how it really works, what it really involves. There is a huge curiosity surrounding it. This is, therefore, very much *our* perfectly imperfect story. At its simplest, our experience of homeschooling is a real one.

Warts and all. We've stumbled through it. We've felt the fear (indeed we still feel the fear) but we are also seeing the results and are coming out the other side with what we'd describe as some pretty spectacular results, in the form of our two daughters.

We want to stress from the outset that this book is not a 'how-to manual', telling you all the right and wrong ways of approaching homeschooling. Instead, this aims to be a book that candidly shares in the ups and downs of our strange but wonderful journey trying to educate our kids outside the conventional schooling system. There will be practical suggestions that have worked for *our* girls and suggestions on what might work for other kids. We will discuss the concept of 'radical de-schooling', a phrase that made Mark break out in a Covid-19-style fever, and a concept that can reveal just how co-dependent not only our kids are on the system, but also us as parents too, by essentially stopping all formal learning for a considerable amount of time at the beginning of a child's homeschooling journey. Think of it as a form of educative cold turkey!

A key part of our approach to homeschooling has been an acceptance of possible failure and this is really important to mention. We're not claiming to be the beacons of homeschooling, nor do we have all the answers. Many choices we've made were the wrong ones, many others were right in none of the ways we expected them to be, and some of the greatest decisions we've ever made could never have been described as decisions in the first place! We have simply stumbled here, fallen there and found ourselves in the unlikeliest of places, turning circumstances into opportunities to learn something new and meaningful. We will share in these failures.

At no stage have we ever pretended to be teachers; we have only ever positioned ourselves as grown-up people who are themselves still learning about the world and who want to learn alongside our girls. If there was any theory to what we've done, any strategy, we would have to sum this up by the phrase 'only connect' as used by the author E. M. Forster, which means only by connecting everything you experience in life to something else can any meaning, understanding or joy be had.

This book is all about the connections we've tried to make between ourselves and our girls' learning and the connections we've failed to make. But fundamentally this is a book for anyone who *feels* that the system isn't serving their child well, wants to do something about it, and wants to reconnect their child back to the essential idea of what it means to learn. Learning can be fun and that's not a bad thing. Homeschooling has the potential to connect you to your child in a way you could have only ever dreamed of, but more importantly, it will connect your child to the world in a truly meaningful and creative way.

By this stage we may be experienced homeschoolers of our *own* children, but we would never suggest we could

expertly educate anyone else's kids. We can suggest strategies for trusting yourself, your instincts, and trusting
your kids. But remember this is about you and *your*
relationship with your own unique child. We hope that
by reading this book you will feel more equipped and less
at sea if you ever decide to homeschool your child. We
will walk and talk you through the process of taking your
child out of school, discuss the groups and communities
that are out there to help, and explain how at certain
times we used the syllabus to help us and how we departed
from it at others. We will highlight and share in the fears
and doubts we all feel as homeschooling parents. We also
hope that if, in the unlikely event of, say, a global
pandemic (!!), or, more realistically, your child is deeply
unhappy or struggling at school, you don't need to face
homeschooling on your own.

## No such thing as a perfect education

Remember, there is no perfect education for your
child. School (even when a child 'successfully'
passes all the way through it from ages three to
eighteen), is rarely a seamless or smooth
experience. Neither is homeschooling. It offers up
a different range of challenges. But one thing it
undoubtedly does is places your child centre-stage

for their own education. If nothing else, this book will remind you that you are not alone in your journey. Which is why it is not a 'how to do homeschooling perfectly' book. That would be a bum steer. Instead, consider this an honest, warts-and-all imperfectly perfect guide to accompany you on your own journey, should you find yourself in your kitchen wondering how to teach chemistry to your twelve year old!

Every morning and evening in bed, we often ask ourselves: are we succeeding at this homeschooling lark? What *are* we doing? Nothing is more important to us than the education of our kids. Taking full responsibility for their learning is frightening because it matters so much to us. Just because they don't go to school doesn't mean that all bets are off. Quite the opposite. When you think about it, it's relatively easy to drop your kids at the school gates every day and trust that the school will do what's needed for them. When you wake up as a homeschooler, you are responsible for every single bit of learning your child will receive that day. But our measuring sticks to gauge success or failure are very different to those in most other households (and this is something you'll need to adapt to if you decide homeschooling is the best route for your family).

Whereas most parents and children can rely on the

grades achieved at SATs, GCSEs and A Levels as barometers of success, we don't have any obvious markers because we've essentially turned our back on the system. Our gauges of success are more subtle and less academic. It can be a lonelier route and one that comes with judgement, but the one thing we are both in absolute agreement about is that at the point each of our girls moved into homeschooling, the mainstream education system, as it then existed, had profoundly failed them and we felt we had no other choice available to us.

Has it been a success? Did we make the right decisions at the right time? Were we qualified in any way whatsoever to take responsibility for our kids' educations? Well, despite many wobbles on the way, we are just about arriving at a point where we might (at a push) say yes!

We hope this book will be a practical, inspirational and down-to-earth resource for parents who are interested in understanding how homeschooling works, written by parents who have been through it all. We want this book to be the book we would have bought way back at the beginning – one that is not afraid to share in the struggles and setbacks, and be realistic in its ambitions for both homeschooled children and their parents. We read many books, joined many closed Facebook groups and attended countless meetings with other homeschooling parents, but there was no *one* single go-to resource that wasn't afraid to admit that homeschooling is as much a 'finding out' process as it is a case of simply using this or that technique.

In fact, many of the successes of homeschooling are only ever discernible with the benefit of hindsight.

•

It's important to note that as we write we are in the middle of the coronavirus crisis, and while by the time you're reading this, we may well be out 'the other side', this crisis has in many ways aimed a much-needed spotlight on the very essence of what learning and education are meant to be. Coronavirus has thrown down a gauntlet for *all* parents; challenging us to think on our feet, forcing us all to try and find the teachers deep within. However, while the crisis has made many parents go into a state of unbridled panic, it has also, more importantly (we believe), thrown up an enormous *opportunity*.

Not an opportunity to simply pull all our kids out of school and live our lives like, say, the family in the movie *Captain Fantastic* (in which a family lives in the woods, growing their own food, learning to hunt as well as read, essentially living their lives off the grid.) Not at all.

What we mean is that we have potentially been gifted a *huge* opportunity to essentially do a much-needed 'audit' on what it is we want and need from our education system for our children, and what do our children *need* for themselves?

When we first saw images on social media and in the press of families trying to recreate the *exact* classroom conditions of school within their lounges and kitchens, we both wanted to scream, 'STOOPPPPPPP!' When we heard stories of children and parents replicating the school timetable we were taken back to those early days of fear and worry when we too - against our wills but in very different circumstances - found the education of our children landing in our own laps.

In many ways, when we take our children to the school gate, hand them over to the teachers and turn to leave, we are essentially crossing our fingers, gritting our teeth and hoping for the best. We have no real, intimate sense of how they will be taught for the day; we have no real sense of how they will socialise or how they will be encouraged to socialise; we simply cross our fingers and *hope*. In many ways we 'let go' when we leave our children at the school gates - and there's a good reason for this. We have to work, we have to earn money, we have to live, we lack the expertise to teach, we don't have the childcare.

## The easy option?

To take responsibility for your children's education is (contrary to all those stereotypes that still prevail) not the easiest option. It is in many ways by far the toughest. And yet, it can also be the most rewarding too.

What we will be discussing in this book is the very personal journey we have taken with both our girls as they moved from conventional schooling towards homeschooling. But (and it is a *huge* but) we are *not* anti-school. If we *are* anti anything, we are anti *bad* schools, and we are anti huge parts of an educational system that bizarrely loses sight of the child in all the administrative noise. We are anti any institution that doesn't recognise or acknowledge that a school environment can be incredibly difficult for some kids. We are anti schools that wilfully turn a blind eye to bullying. We are anti schools run by heads who care more about the fees or the SATs results than they do about the small human beings they are in charge of and care for for a staggering thirty to forty hours a week.

Throughout this book we will share our thoughts on how we think the current coronavirus crisis could well shake the traditional school system to its core. The system as it has been structured is no longer fit for purpose and it simply doesn't cater to kids who want to leave early and pursue more vocational careers or interests. The system presupposes that learning is all about getting grades and passing exams. The pressure comes not only from schools but also from parents. An increasing number of kids are essentially peer pressured by society into thinking they must go into higher education when many of the degrees they go on to take aren't even appropriate for them, their skillset or what they'll later go on to pursue in life. More often than not, the decision to go to uni is not particularly well thought-out, precisely because kids are forced into making such a *huge* decision about what *feels* like the rest of their lives, at such an early age. The idea that choosing your GCSEs at just fourteen to sixteen in order to determine what you might be eligible to study at university is flawed. Who on earth knows (or should know) at just sixteen what they're going to want to do with the rest of their lives?

Going into this period of enforced family isolation – and having to take responsibility for their children's learning – many parents will realise and see for themselves how stressed and pressurised their kids (and teachers) are. Many of our daughter's friends who do go to school talk about only learning what they need to in order to pass exams, and then promptly forgetting what they've learned once they've sat the exam. Is this really what learning is about?

> *All children have talents and we squander them ruthlessly.*
>
> Sir Ken Robinson

The system has lost sight of the child and that is a devastating shame. In a lot of cases, it has made learning a null and void concept because everyone is simply aiming for the same target. Where mainstream learning takes the qualification as the end point and then works its way back to find the child; homeschooling takes the child as the starting point without too much focus on any specific end point. The end point is kept open.

After all, no one should hit a certain age in their life and decide it's time to stop learning. Did *you* stop learning at the point school finished, or did the 'real' learning, a different type of learning, kick in once you'd left?

In lockdown, there are countless parents seeing their children experience something close to an educational form of 'cold turkey', with all their targets, regulations, deadlines, grades and predicted grades having temporarily or even permanently vanished off the radar. Surely, the system cannot keep charging forward in the same manner, with the potency and relevance of GCSEs and A Levels appearing to diminish almost overnight? Although the coronavirus crisis will undoubtedly go down in history as a bizarre blip, we strongly believe that in *any* downturn there is *always* the chance to re-evaluate things.

We need to ask questions we've perhaps been too scared to ask for a long time. Why do we *only* believe in GCSEs, A Levels and degrees as the standard educational narrative? Why is *everything* geared towards going to university? Why is learning measured in principally academic ways? What system have we signed up to, and is it necessarily the *only* one available to us when it comes to educating our children?

# Our individual school stories

Most parents or parents-to-be naturally want their kids to get the best education available. But the vast majority of us form our ideas on what that is from our own positive and/or negative experiences of education. Most childhood memories revolve around school and everyone, on reflection, can remember good times *and* bad. So, there is always something to either conform to, or rebel against.

Schooling (and the types of school parents opt for) tend to run through families like a stick of rock. Tradition runs deep. Educational habits are hard to break, and all too often we as parents assume that our choices are limited by law, location and finances.

For us, as children, we had very different experiences of school. We come from families that had very different attitudes to education and learning. Neither one was better or worse than the other, but they *were* different; and in their different ways both experiences have really helped mould the type of homeschooling parents we have unwittingly become.

## Clues from your past

We would suggest for any parent considering homeschooling, or anyone who simply feels the mainstream system isn't delivering or working for their kids, to cast your minds back and remember precisely what it was you liked and what it was you hated about *your* schooling and learning experience. Not only can it be quite cathartic, but, like a detective, you can also sift through it for clues and ideas on how you could better support your child's learning. Which teachers stood out? Which subjects did you love and which did you hate? How big were the class sizes? What were your biggest worries at school? When were your worst of times, and when were your best?

Although people are keen to define and divide schools into different types and camps, we have to keep reiterating: we have *never* been anti-school. Our approach to Maddie and Kiki's learning is something we like to refer to as 'Complementary Learning' (a little bit like Complementary Medicine). We are not closed off to conventional learning, and indeed we lean on it a lot at times, but we are also *not* slave to it, and it's this part of the equation which has very much defined our home-schooling experience.

By mapping out *your* school story (including all the good things and the bad), not only can you better understand the decisions you've made thus far about your own children's educations, but hopefully it will also give you some clarity and renewed purpose about making better decisions for the future. You'll be surprised. We found the process of writing our own school stories a useful and incredibly revealing exercise. It was also an unexpectedly emotional one. Education, whether it be our own as children, or that of our kids, is one of (if not) *the* most significant factors in our lives. It defines almost everything else in our lives.

So, what were our individual experiences of school and learning, and how did they mould or influence our attitudes to Maddie and Kiki's education?

## Nadia

*My father once said, 'Every parent should know that after the first day you wave your child off to school, they return changed forever. Something is lost.' As I think about how* my schooling affected my decisions around homeschooling Maddie and Kiki, perhaps his words laid a seed or two . . .

It's safe to say that from the get-go I didn't like rules. I didn't understand them . . . I didn't really see the point of them.

My first memory of school was walking home from nursery with my mum bemoaning the fact that when the teacher had asked me what I wanted to drink (lemon or orange squash) I had asked for Turkish coffee and had been given short shrift. The class thought it was hilarious. My parents thought this was hilarious. I didn't. My pride had been dented. Maybe that single careless rebuff from my first teacher set the tone for my whole schooling life. Who can know? I certainly don't think I helped things. On my second day at nursery I walked in, lifted my skirt as high as I could and announced I had new pants on! As Mark says, things haven't changed much!

After nursery I went to a state primary school. It was a Christian school and my sister Dina and I were the only kids there who hadn't been christened. My mum and dad basically bribed the headmaster with 'a bag of gold' (the headmaster's words, not mine) and a dodgy bottle of 'holy water' from a recent trip to my dad's homeland of Jordan! My parents assure me that they behaved in this scurrilous way simply because it was 'the best school in the area' – a familiar refrain of all parents then and now!

The headmaster of this school was, in my humble opinion, tough. Anyone late for school was punished. It must have worked though: to this day I'm never late, and I can't bear it when others are!

He was a terrifying man. But, I kind of liked him, and he liked me. How strange! Interestingly, my mum says she regrets sending me there as in my second year they began a style of learning called 'family grouping', a teaching method that apparently involved the older children somehow teaching the younger children. Although I have absolutely no memory of this, Mum says that I unfortunately took to it like a duck to water, so completely and committedly inhabiting the role of 'teacher' that I spent the hours I should have been learning teaching the younger ones! God knows what I taught them as I knew diddly squat! All in all, despite the tough headmaster and the very bizarre 'family grouping' method, I enjoyed my time at this school.

When I was about nine, we moved to a bigger house with a bigger garden, and I HATED it. They thought we'd love a big garden, but I just missed my friends and was pretty glum throughout the summer holidays. But there was hope on the horizon with my second primary school! No tough head teachers running the show this time. A classic brilliant state primary school. The headmaster Mr Woods had the kindest, saddest eyes I'd ever seen. I felt safe there. I struggled a bit with the written work but excelled in group discussion and reading. But a year in, I started to get terrible headaches, and a trip to the opticians revealed that I had probably never seen anything on the blackboard. I was very short-sighted!

At All Saints, I was a happy-go-lucky kid, but if I'm honest

I only did the minimum amount of work. For me, school was all about the socialising, even back then! I couldn't really see the point of a lot of what I was learning. I had a severe case of 'butterfly brain', and because I didn't really take to the academic side of things, my parents were at a loss when it came to deciding which secondary school I should go to.

They simply assumed I would go to the 'very good' all-girls grammar school that my eldest sister Dina went to. But, horror of horrors, I failed the interview, which was a huge shock and one, I hasten to add, I still haven't fully recovered from. We all assumed that because I was the confident, opinionated one, I'd be able to walk and talk my way through the forty-minute interview with the headmistress. Sadly, it didn't go according to plan. She obviously saw me for what I was: a precocious little twerp who would probably never amount to much! So, Mum and Dad were forced to regroup and rethink.

Now, it's important to say, my parents weren't anti state school at all, but unfortunately, we didn't live in a great area, so the schools on offer were dire and they were reluctant to 'throw me to the wolves!' So, bless them, they entered me for the entrance exam for a local 'posh' private school. I had to sit a two-hour exam covering most subjects, and it's fair to say none of us thought I even stood a chance! How wrong could we all have been? I actually got in!! (They were probably short on cash that year!)

I was what could only be described as a well-behaved rebel at school. Never really getting into any major trouble but still always skirting around the rules doing what the hell I liked. That said, teachers always seemed to like me, but God knows why! I was a nightmare at handing in homework, and often played the clown, reducing the class to hysterics. But bless their hearts, they saw potential in me. A potential that, to be honest, I never fully realised for them. In retrospect, I feel quite bad about this! I had a great opportunity, the luxury of a private education and yet, If I'm honest, I was actively a terrible student.

It must have been so frustrating for all the grown-ups in my childhood, as I was very confident and could hold my own in most discussions both within the classroom and with my large and extremely verbose extended family, but I just couldn't translate it into my academic performance.

I'm pretty sure if we'd known about ADHD back then I would have been diagnosed, for sure. I have always had a strange body and mind that just can't settle on any one thing for very long. It's as if my brain misses a beat (and therefore often the point!) and so concentration has always been a challenge for me.

I loved all those subjects that related to the human condition; English, RE and drama. Basically, give me a subject that we would spend time in class discussing rather than putting pen to paper, and I was good to go. I was a Loose Woman even back then! Indeed, to this day, I never make or refer to notes when I'm filming, or on live telly, or writing! (e.g. I will definitely be getting Mark to go through all my contributions in this book!!)

So, I spent two years (quite miserably) at an all-girls

school in Streatham in my snot-green uniform and nuns' flat brown brogues, knowing that I wasn't quite firing on all cylinders. I hated it. I hated the uniform, the smell, the stuck-up teachers. I would silently weep in physics and chemistry I hated it so much. I hated the boiled cabbage lunches, the dark corridors and the general jolly-hockey-sticks atmosphere. I'm not exaggerating when I say I felt like I was serving a sentence for a crime I didn't commit. I felt suffocated and bewildered, like my life was running away from me (I was a drama queen even back then). But I plodded along ducking and diving. I had great friends and, as with the whole of my life, they're what got me through the lonnnnggg boring days. My biggest problem was that I didn't know where I was heading. I didn't know what I wanted to be. It felt like everyone else in my class had a clear ambition and they were studying all the right subjects to realise their dreams.

I'm afraid, and maybe a little bit ashamed, to say that at this point in my life (you could say the most crucial point of life), I just hadn't discovered a love for the simple act of learning. But then . . . it was the first night of my school play. I had never performed in front of an audience before, and the thrill was overwhelming. From the second I stepped on stage and got a huge laugh (which with hindsight was probably more to do with the fact I had a handlebar moustache stuck to my face, not because of any great comic ability!) something deep inside me clicked. A show-off's dream had just come true.

However, the real epiphany about what I was going to

do with the rest of my life hit me at exactly the same time I bumped into my mum. She looked at me with a look of utter shock and gasped, 'Nadia you were really, really good! You really made me laugh!' Little did she realise that upon uttering that simple sentence, my poor mum had unwittingly unleashed the beast! I had found my calling. I knew absolutely what I wanted to do and what I wanted to be. From that point on I wanted to be an actress, and nothing was going to stop me.

Fast forward two weeks later, it's seven a.m. and I'm standing in my parents' bedroom waving an application form, demanding they let me audition for the Italia Conti stage school. I'd researched the whole thing without my parents knowing.

Bless them they were half asleep, and had their guard down, and at first, they just laughed at me! This was the most important moment of my life and they were laughing! So (with a great sense of drama) I calmly threatened to throw myself out the window if they didn't let me audition.

Bleary eyed, reluctantly (secretly thinking that there was no way I would get in as it was a tiny performing arts school and thousands auditioned every year) they said yes. Luckily for me they'd underestimated my determination. I took the audition (aged thirteenish) and was offered a place the same day. My poor parents. They couldn't say no now. But as far as I was concerned, my life was just about to get started!

My first day was an absolute eye-opener; a hundred and twenty children ALL wanting to be at this particular school *more than anything else in the world. I cannot describe how different this felt. This wasn't what school was supposed to be like was it? You're not supposed to ENJOY being at school. It was meant to be hard work, drudgery, a task to be completed, an experience to be endured - wasn't it?! The energy and excitement at Italia Conti were palpable.*

*I was with my people. In every corridor there was someone learning lines, doing the splits or singing their lungs out. Yes, there were plenty of bitchy competitive stares, but because I'd decided this was where I was meant to be nothing was going to put me off!*

*I stayed at Italia Conti for the next three years. Our days were split into two: academic subjects in the morning (there was no chemistry or physics and ONLY arithmetic), while the afternoons were spent dancing, acting and singing. I'd finally found my tribe and I loved every second of it! But I hasten to add this doesn't mean I became the model studious student at all!! I had a ball, and I learnt about having drive and ambition - but don't for a second think I wasn't still a skiver (I was!).*

*I had a great few years there and really did love the atmosphere and the people, but the academic side of things still bored me rigid, and I fought against the very concept of being told how to learn. At parents' evenings Mum kept being told I had so much potential - and then the head said, 'I have a terrible fear it could all go very wrong for Nadia - and she could amount to nothing more than a dilettante.' I eventually left school for good at fifteen, equipped with just* one O Level in English Language. My parents, seeing how restless I was becoming, came up with the bizarre and possibly illegal plan of giving me the equivalent money that they would have paid in school fees to travel and learn the 'lessons of life'. Not even an adult, there I was heading off to the airport with a ticket to the Middle East.

I suppose, at the time, my parents would have seemed half mad, but looking back it would be fair to say that they had the homeschooling bug without even realising it. In fact, it's only really fully dawning on me as I sit here writing this: they instinctively knew that unless they let me fly the schooling nest and find my own way, I was more than likely going to go completely off the rails! They realised that some-times the best thing to do with a rebellious child is to break the rules. Go against the flow. Thank GOD!! This vital decision was absolutely the making of me.

My first stop was Amman, Jordan (my father's homeland), where I moved into my uncle's house and knuckled down to work. I worked my arse off helping to run his creative arts centre, teaching dance and drama. Extraordinary when you think I was just fifteen with zero qualifications and a long winding queue of teachers behind me who almost definitely thought I wouldn't add up to anything. In fact, the women I used to teach while out there still ask after me whenever my parents visit Jordan! I stuck at it for almost a year before flying to Boston in the USA to look at drama colleges. I had proved every one of my teachers wrong, I was already 'in the world' forging my own chaotic way, and I was sixteen!

## Mark

*Socially, I loved primary school. Loved it. It was a state primary in Ladbroke Grove, London, during the mid-seventies. It was essentially a prefabricated building that was so temporary in its nature that walls would literally fall down on us in the middle of class.*

*I was captain of the football team, I fell in 'love' (or so I thought) for the first time with Lilith, my nickname was alternately Bladderley or Bladders (I always needed the loo), and my school report consistently described me as an incredibly popular and bright kid.*

*It was a brilliant time. The sweltering hot summer of 1976, watching our playground melt, sticking our fingers into the gooey tarmac, hearing stories of blockbuster movies over in the USA! My most abiding memories are of a sunny and funny time. Sweating (I was a sweaty-headed footballer and ran around a lot) and laughing were the order of the day.*

*At home there was just me and my mother. No dad. No siblings. Mum was a single parent, and she worked full time in a college library. Most of my days were spent either at school or at playcentre (the afterschool club that ran till six p.m. every day except Friday). I had the time of my life . . . ruled the roost . . . and was one of those annoying blonde-haired boys who didn't stop asking question after question after question. I felt safe and secure there. Sometimes more secure than at home.*

It ran like this until I was about eight or nine, when my mother came out as gay. Not literally, I hasten to add; she never sat me down and said, 'Mark, I'm gay.' It just sort of evolved and I simply got used to her having girlfriends rather boyfriends. Back in 1978/79 attitudes to homosexuality weren't particularly progressive, and ever so slowly, as the word spread about my mother, my social world started to implode a bit. Friends stopped coming over for sleepovers. My mum was described as 'that weirdo', in fact, other kids' parents actually came to our front door and hurled terrible abuse at my mother and her then girlfriend.

It's safe to say the wind was taken out of my sails a bit. I couldn't see what was wrong with what my mother was doing, and yet I was being met with either real hostility, or a peculiar stand-offishness from many of my closest friends. I muscled on and tried to ignore the noise, helped greatly by a very kind teacher (also a Mr Woods) who must have felt some degree of paternal protection towards me. I felt he had my back. He would reach out to my mother whenever he thought I was down or behaving erratically and he flagged up concerns with my health (mental and physical).

Mr Woods was also the person who introduced me to the magical possibility of filmmaking, by simply helping me and a friend set up a stop-frame animation unit in the sports equipment cupboard, where we made an animation and projected it in front of the whole class. It was just a round paper ball falling off a cliff – but the wonder and excitement

I felt at seeing what I could create has never left me to this day. A love of film was quite literally born in that cramped, sports equipment cupboard.

If things could be described as fraught towards the end of primary school, secondary school in 1981 was an entirely different struggle. As I said, back then, sadly, having a gay mother wasn't particularly easy, especially not at what was then the biggest comprehensive school in London (Holland Park). I really struggled to settle in to secondary school. I never felt very cool, I was always a bit of a loner, I even got drunk in class (laying the groundwork for later alcoholism) and I was often rude to teachers. My studies between eleven and fourteen were anything but impressive. To the outside observer it was increasingly clear that I was on the road to failure.

Fortunately, though, as clichéd as it might sound, love sort of saved the day!!! I fell in 'love' at fourteen, something which, in retrospect, I can see changed the course of my entire education. Both being loners and neither of us knowing our fathers, me and my then girlfriend (Jane) drifted through school on the fringes of things. There was still a lot of homophobia about my mum, a lot of scuffles, but my girlfriend and I were also marked out as the weird ones who 'were in love', and we kind of got left alone. I also slowly began to discover (as O Levels headed towards me) that if I was willing to put in the effort with schoolwork, I could get good grades, and teachers would keep talking about things like A Levels!

*Like someone out of a corny eighties movie, wearing awful clothes and holding Jane's hand throughout, I began to fashion myself an escape route to something new. A mystical place my grandmother kept talking about, and that my teachers kept mentioning the further I progressed through school . . . university.*

*The idea of university was hard-wired into me by my nan. My mother never went, my grandparents never went. Instead, I was instilled with the idea that going into higher education was something worth aspiring to, not as a means to 'Keep up with Joneses', but as an opportunity that my nan and grandad (who were essentially my co-parents) saw as 'Going past the Joneses'. I'm convinced my push to university was a class and snobbery thing given to me by my grandparents. However, thanks to the teachers I had in the seventies and eighties in my state schools, I also discovered an absolute passion for the three most important things in my life – English, art and film.*

*So, with the broadest of brush strokes I went to primary school, secondary school and university. Pretty standard really.*

*But there were several aspects to this otherwise simple journey that I now realise were not only crucial to how my adult life developed, but also strongly informed many of the schooling decisions I've made as a parent, good and bad. At the age of ten, I was encouraged by my primary headteacher to pursue (with the support of my mother) a scholarship to a reputable private school (he believed I would get in easily).*

But for political reasons, my mother said she didn't want me to go there and instead wanted me to go to Holland Park, which had a reputation for being a free-thinking, liberal-minded artsy school (in terms of its teaching but not, as it turned out, in terms of the bullying). Although I obviously did as my mother wanted me to, this sliding-doors moment has always stayed with me. To this day I entertain countless 'what ifs' regarding this junction early in my life - and it was a very significant part of my decision in wanting Maddie and Kiki-Bee to go to a good (potentially fee-paying) highly academic school.

But running contrary to this very formal, conventional and quite conservative attitude to learning and schooling, probably the biggest influence on my more creative attitudes to learning were moulded by the countless remarkable teachers I encountered in the state system of the seventies and eighties; a time when teachers had the freedom to teach creatively and instinctively. Indeed, when I now look back over my own learning story I realise that I couldn't quite shake the sense of the benefits of a highly structured academic education even while I was being liberated by the free-flowing liberal hippiedom of all those teachers who essentially broke every rule in the teaching handbook and managed to help me realise that learning was about far more than just grades and exams and tests. To this day, I am eternally grateful to those weird, whacked out, probably (in this day and age) inappropriate teachers who were interested in ideas and the minds and hearts of us kids, rather than hitting quotas, being high enough in league tables and being assessed to within an inch of our lives. English teachers would show us films, history teachers would perform poetry, politics teachers would encourage us to self-publish magazines; it was a melting pot of creative thinking where the defining edges of academic subjects were purposefully erased and deconstructed. I can remember each of those teachers who transformed my comprehension of learning for ever: Mr Kruger, Mr Warwick, Ms Vass and Mr McDonald. They all taught me how every single subject could feed into another subject . . . It was sometimes utterly mind-blowing and liberating . . . but also scary!

As I discovered at the age of sixteen with E. M. Forster, everything is connected to everything else! Our job as humans is to simply and 'only connect'.

While this hippy, flower-power approach to learning was going on at school, there was also a vital other component of my learning that was even more unconventional. My mother, a librarian, was a brilliant supplier of books. There were books everywhere when I was a kid. She was also a very, very young single mum who perhaps allowed me a little too much freedom as a child. But I have strong memories of her pulling me out of school under the guise of a dentist's appointment and then taking me with her to see all manner of foreign films at a cinema in Portobello Market. Half the time I didn't know what was going on, but it all seeped in. Around the age of nine or ten, I struck up a friendship with my babysitter, who was a dear friend of my mother's but who also happened to be an abstract painter. He was my art teacher until the day he died when I was just twenty, and to this day his tutelage helps me when teaching the girls about artists.

So, as you can probably tell this unique blending of structure and creative chaos in my education and learning was in its own way a form of Complementary Learning.

Yes, I was going to a building every day that happened to be called a school, but my learning was despite the building. My learning was only a result of countless teachers and other people in my life breaking with convention and essentially breaking the rules.

Given the fact that the social aspect of school was the part I enjoyed the least, it was all the creative-learning stuff that really fired me up. I quite simply fell in love with the idea that there were apparently absolutely no limits to what you could learn or how you could learn it. But, most importantly of all, I grew to fully appreciate the interconnectedness of so many different disciplines and subjects from a young age.

This profound realisation helped steer me with increasing speed and hunger through my A Levels, a BA in English, Art & Film, an MA in Filmmaking and even the beginnings of a PhD . . . At every single stage I was blessed with tutors, teachers and lecturers who were all united by one dominant idea: BREAK THE RULES!

All of this (I hasten to add) I have only come to realise slowly over the years, which would perhaps account for why, when me and Nadia were faced with our own girls' educations,

*I chose to zero in on just one element of my learning experience. The bit that had left me with so many 'what ifs'. Why didn't my mother let me try for that scholarship?*

*I felt a need all these years later to right a wrong, and so private or prep school had taken on huge proportions in my mind. Put simply, I wanted my girls to have the opportunity I felt I had been denied.*

●

As we've said, the highs and lows surrounding both of our very different and contrasting schooling and learning experiences have been crucially important when it comes to the decisions we've made regarding Maddie and Kiki's educations. Not only have our individual learning experiences informed some of our worst decisions, they've also been a source of great inspiration for some of our best ones too!

If you are in *any way* toying with the idea of home-schooling your kids or, at the very least, adjusting and transforming the ways in which your kids learn, we would heartily encourage, as the very first step, for you to sit down after reading this and try to write down your own blow-by-blow account of your school life. If you have a partner, get them to do the same. Write a vigorously honest inventory of your own schooling experience at each stage of your childhood. List the good things and the bad and then read them back to yourselves and each other.

Who inspired you the most? Why? How? What did you hate the most? How could it have been made better? Take yourself back in time, interrogate the received wisdoms surrounding the type of school you went to. Whether it was a boarding school, day school, grammar school, convent school, state school . . . whatever. Why did *your* parents choose that school for *you?* Ask them. Consider the reasons behind your own schooling preferences. Has modern-day life shifted considerably since the days your parents chose where to send you? Are you simply going with the same choice because it's easy? Or because it's what's expected? We met surprising resistance from some of the older members of our family when we elected to homeschool, so be sure to be fearlessly honest and frank in your assessment of your family's schooling story!

# Before homeschooling

## Why did we privately educate our girls?

> If you're not prepared to be wrong, you'll never come up with anything original.
>
> Sir Ken Robinson

Now you've got some background on where we were coming from educationally, let's take ourselves back to the beginning of our own homeschooling journey. A journey that essentially began with our very first well-meaning decision to send our girls Maddie and Kiki-Bee to a fee-paying prep school. We both agreed on the decision, but we had both arrived at it for different reasons.

At its simplest, we felt that choosing the *best* type of education meant you *paid* for it.

We were about to find out just how unprepared we were to be *wrong*!!

## Mark

*Where me and Nadia connected on the private-school front was over the view that it was aspirational. On some level, we both hoped that private school would open up opportunities and skills for our girls that we had perhaps missed. How wrong could we have been? The decision to send first Maddie and then Kiki to the same prep school was compounded by the fact that I had had to take a back seat in the educations of my two eldest daughters, Isobel and Fleur. With Maddie and Kiki, I wanted to be certain we made the best decision we could for them both, in a way that I'd felt slightly locked out of with my eldest.*

*When I first became a parent back in 1993, I used to push Issy past the local fee-paying girls school and hover in the drive looking all misty eyed at the building thinking, 'One day, Issy. One day you'll get the choices and opportunities I missed out on.' In retrospect, I realise I was lucky not to get arrested, standing there as I did, looking balefully at the school grounds!*

*However, our hands were also forced towards a fee-paying school by one other enormous parenting dilemma: at the time* we felt (rightly or wrongly) that all the state schools in our neighbourhood weren't right for Maddie. We also worried that with both of us working in the media and Nadia being instantly recognisable, we would feel a little vulnerable about the girls going to the local state primary. Were we being snobby? Probably. But as parents we sometimes feel things irrationally, and back then we probably felt that we needed some added 'insurances' when it came to the girl's learning. So what better than a fee-paying prep school to prepare them and us for life?!

So, we hit upon a good local prep school. Not the poshest. Not necessarily one of the best. Not one of the most expensive. But a good reputable one. We sent Maddie, and by-and-large her journey through nursery, infants and junior was relatively positive. Or so we thought.

The same, sadly, could not be said when we eventually sent our youngest girl Kiki-Bee.

Almost immediately, Kiki-Bee's experience of school was where the cracks started to show in our idyllic and slightly naive attitude to both her and Maddie's educations.

## Nadia

I truly believe that the single worst choice we ever made for both our daughters was sending them to a highly academic private school. If I had my time again, I would almost definitely have sent them to the local state primary, regardless of reputation or where it was in the league tables. I must say from the outset that the school we chose wasn't a bad school, it was just the wrong school for Maddie and Kiki. Although Maddie was obviously the first to go (when she was almost four years of age), we only really started to become aware of a mismatch between the school and our girls when Kiki-Bee went.

The first day we took Kiki to school was not a happy day for me. She was as cute as a button in her teeny uniform and her tightly (there was cursing) braided plaits. Kiki-Bee was what they call a summer baby, which meant that she was a whole year younger than most of the other children in her class. And she really was. I can still remember her hanging onto my legs as she peered from behind them at her teacher and classmates. Every fibre of my being told me to pick her up and run home. As lovely as the school and all the teachers were, I knew she wasn't ready for the huge leap from mud pies and all-day play to full-on lessons with a lot of time sitting still on her bum! It will always be a major regret of mine that I didn't follow my instinct. Maybe if she had had one more year at home, like most of the other kids did, she wouldn't have had to go through the horrors that she later did. But, if I'm honest, this would have been very difficult for me, as I was a working mum. To this day, I feel intensely guilty about this.

If there's one thing I've learned over the years, it's to trust your gut instinct when it comes to your kids. Every time I haven't listened to my sixth sense in relation to our girls,

I've always regretted it, and throughout Kiki's time at school I repeatedly ignored not just my sixth sense, but my seventh and eighth too.

Firstly, I would like to say that Kiki's school was, in many ways, a lovely environment. It was small, friendly, had some smashing teachers and most of the children there seemed to be very happy. Kiki had the kindest of teachers in nursery, and she was immediately taken under the wing of a teacher who was sympathetic to the fact that she was younger than most of the other children in her class.

However, unfortunately, after only a few weeks into her first term, we received a panic-stricken phone call from the school telling us that Kiki had tripped on a carpet and split her head open – blood everywhere. I can't help but feel it was an omen.

In these early days, although Kiki made friends, enjoyed the sandpit, played with tadpoles, loved the dressing-up box, etc., she was actually desperate to be at home. The hustle and bustle and noise were too much for her as she was very shy and always craved the quiet. Poor kid with me as a mother! Six months into nursery, we began to feel that the nursery teachers were worried about her. They didn't say this out loud, but I could tell by the way they were suggesting 'various activities' for her to 'try at home' that they were already categorising her as 'a bit behind'. I would always smile politely and nod like a crazy woman, making all sorts of promises, while privately thinking to myself, 'She's ONLY THREE, she's not doing blooming homework!' In my mind

*I didn't want her to be at bloody school yet anyway, so I certainly wasn't going to give her homework to do too! The poor thing was always knackered by the time she got home and desperate to just hang out and play with her big sis.*

*When I look back, I feel like I was a bit of an idiot. To be fair to the teachers, they were trying to help us help Kiki, fully aware that reception and year 1 would otherwise be very challenging for her - and us.*

## Mark

*I remember this earliest period of Kiki being at school as extremely stressful. Through no real fault of the school, I felt quite quickly as though our girls were being sent to a place that couldn't (structurally) cater for their more nuanced needs. Maddie had already been at the school for a few years by the time Kiki went to nursery, and although she was a more naturally extroverted and gregarious girl (she could hold her own, she wasn't shy, when she cried, her voice could be heard in the neighbouring London borough), like Nadia, my sixth sense was picking up that beneath the social surface things weren't quite stacking up academically.*

*Over time, we would discover that I should have listened to those inner voices, but at the time Kiki went to school, Maddie appeared to be having a largely positive experience. So, in for a penny, in for a pound. Two sisters going to the same school made a lot of sense. While we were still a few years away from discovering that Maddie was hiding an inability to slot into the school's very academic slipstream, Kiki's struggles were far more obvious from the get-go.*

*The terrible dilemma for any parent when it comes to our children not liking, enjoying or taking to school, is trying to work out the dividing line between what we should allow our kids to go through (i.e. all children cry about going to school, many kids are shy, not all kids find all elements of school easy), and at what point we need to step in and help, or nudge things in a different direction.*

*With Kiki, quite early on, there was a sense that the structure, even the very voices of the teachers, was something she found anathema to easy learning. The other dilemma for nearly all parents is whether to assume that these things will simply sort themselves out. I would often be at work, and if Nadia described how upset Kiki was, I would try and temper my distant fears with the thought that 'this is what all kids go through, to some extent'. I would consciously say to Nadia, 'this is sadly part of the process', 'this will rectify itself eventually'. But every time I said it, I secretly doubted whether this was a) the right to thing to say, or b) the right thing to assume. It's a problem for every single parent, and to be honest, the politics of the playground only ever served to make me think we needed to be even tougher with Kiki. Surely, if we just kept pushing her, eventually we would be able to let go of her hand and she would find her own way. Wouldn't she? The peer pressure between parents in the playground was always intense, and although it was never something that sat easily with me and Nadia, we always struggled to disentangle ourselves from the guilt and fear we'd often feel after talking with other parents.*

*If we didn't feel like we belonged in the playground (with other parents talking about a million and one extra-curricular activities, countless tutors, skiing trips etc. etc.) how on earth were our girls supposed to slot into this highly competitive environment?*

## Nadia

*Before Kiki went to school, we were extremely blessed with the fact that our girls got on brilliantly. They liked each other, and we had encouraged them from day one to play, play, play and then play some more. We didn't teach them to read. We didn't have them writing out sums, entering spelling-bees, taking part in Lego tournaments, or joining swimming clubs. Our thinking was that they would be off to school soon enough and that there would be plenty of time for formal learning when they were older. There was zero hot-housing for us and whatever the opposite of a Tiger Mum was, well, that was me, and very proud of ourselves we were too!!*

*BIG MISTAKE!!*

*If I'm brutally honest, a huge part of this was ironically because we were working very hard, earning enough money to afford private school! We learned the hard way that this is NOT how it works when you send your children to private* school, even if they're only starting in nursery. I think it's fair to say Mark and I were a right pair of idiots for not realising this sooner, i.e. before signing the poor blighters up for prep school!

After nursery came reception, and by this time Kiki had sort of accepted that this was her lot, bless her. She wasn't happy about it. Once again, she had a kind teacher, but quite quickly she was struggling with the work. It was around this time we began to realise that her left eye (which had always turned in a tiny bit) was now turning in a lot more. Mark and I have slightly the same squint, so we hadn't thought much of it, but a trip to the opticians revealed some shocking news.

We had had no idea that Kiki had been struggling with very little vision in her left eye. In itself this was devastating enough, but the treatment was going to prove just as devastating for a very young child who was already struggling at school. We were told that she would have to wear a patch on her good eye for eight hours a day to try and get the weak eye to kick in. Kiki was effectively going to be almost blind for her entire school day.

In fact, I remember arriving early one day to pick her up from school and watching her through the glass door of her classroom. Her head was actually on the desk as she tried to see. It broke my heart. How the hell was she going to keep up? It makes me cry remembering this. I feel like the worst mother in the world that I didn't do more to help her. The medical advice was clear that she should wear the patch at school and somehow she wore it all the way through her breaktime too. Of course, this will have come from a good place, the school being told that the patching was the best thing for her. Unbelievably, Kiki only told us this after she left school. Apparently she used to just sit and wait for break to end! This image still tears us apart.

## Mark

The vast majority of Kiki's experience in reception will have quite literally been a blur, accompanied by a cacophony of noise. Knowing the child we have now (she's twelve and sitting alongside me reading), I can only imagine how much this sensory overload in a classroom will have shattered her nerves. She is, by nature, a quiet child. She likes to sit alongside things and observe or listen before jumping in. When she feels comfortable, there's no one louder and more confident, but it takes her time - whether it be approaching an academic subject or a new friendship - time that almost no school can realistically allow for.

As Kiki moved through reception, we made a huge effort to read to the girls a lot. I would often gather up an entire shelf-load of books at a time , pile them on the floor of their bedrooms and exclaim, 'Let's work our way through every single one of them until we have read them all!' And read them all we did. The girls loved the visual challenge and achievement of working our way through these piles a week or a month at a time. Story time in bed with Maddie and Kiki was always fun, and yet it slowly started to become apparent that Kiki couldn't really focus on story time because she was beginning to feel anxious about the following day and going to school.

Extra-curricular activities were a big part of both the girls learning back then. We took them to art galleries every weekend (at age seven, Maddie's favourite painter was Lucian Freud!), we took them to the theatre on a monthly basis, to the Puppet Theatre, to see dance shows, the cinema: I tried to take full advantage of the cultural opportunities a city like London offers up. Okay – we weren't hot-housing them through mental arithmetic and English grammar, but we were trying to maximise their experience of the creative world around them. To be honest, we thought we were doing alright.

## Nadia

As you can imagine, when Kiki moved up to year 1 and started to really 'fall behind', she became more anxious. Even though the teachers said there was no way she could know that she was being given different work, she would tell us herself that she knew very well she was in a different academic set, and that she also felt embarrassed that she wasn't keeping up. All of this, alongside the fact that she could barely see anything, played a huge part in why she eventually became something of a 'school refuser'.

We felt stuck between a rock and a hard place because she was so tired by the time she got home that we couldn't imagine doing extra work with her. It was at this point that she started to really struggle with sleeping. Sleep had always been a bit of an issue but now she would lie awake for hours 'just worrying'. We were then in the vicious cycle where the more anxious she got the less able she was to sleep and the more tired she became the more anxious and on and on. Every single morning, she would cry and beg not to go to school. I would have to force her into her uniform and shoes, hiding my own tears. Day after day after day. We were all exhausted, sad and resigned to the fact that this was probably the way life was going to be for the foreseeable future. She was five years old and we felt we had already failed her.

Every day Kiki would be sent off into a smaller group for children 'who were struggling'. She was grateful for this, because she loved her teacher there and, most importantly, it was quiet. But this separation from the main class did nothing for her self-esteem and she hated it when she had to go back to the normal classroom, with all the noise and competitive atmosphere.

Kiki has since told us that they would always sit her next to the most confident kids who would constantly be shooting their hands into the air and answering everything. To be fair again to the school, they probably did this because they thought it might help her. Sadly, it backfired massively, and left her feeling even more shy than before. She was retreating more and more into her shell. She said she would often sit with tears rolling down her face, silently crying, praying no one would notice, and most importantly praying no one asked her a question. 'I tried really hard not to cry, Mum, because I knew I was really annoying the teacher.' Her telling me this one evening still breaks my heart, especially because I know if I'd been her teacher, I too would have felt frustrated, with twenty other children to look after.

The teachers would ask us over and over again to encourage her to put her hand up, to speak and contribute more during show-and-tell, to open her mouth and become more involved; all these things an absolute nightmare for a shy child.

It's strange, because as I remember these times, I'm reminded of how caught up I was in what the teachers were asking of Kiki. Being an extrovert myself, I too was worried. Coming from my extroverted take on the world, I felt the teachers were right. How would she cope in the big bad outside world if she couldn't put her hand up in class and be heard? As I remember thinking this, I am cringing with embarrassment.

Although I think differently now, I realise just how much the world at large is geared up for those who are the loudest, the brashest, the noisiest (but not necessarily the brightest, cleverest or kindest).

It's taken many years (as the parent of an introverted child) to realise and accept that the world does in fact need many many more shy, quiet thinkers. It is a profound mistake to try and force (or even guide by stealth) a child away from who they truly are.

*I truly believe that many of the anxiety issues that Mark and Kiki have encountered are down to nothing more complicated than the fact that they are both shy people who have been put under remarkable pressure to conform to a loud and extroverted world. The deep irony is, of course, that when they feel safe, no one can be more extroverted than either of them!*

*It's therefore no surprise that a schooling system designed to rapidly 'process' children's heads and hearts has little ability to cater for those kids who need to take things more slowly or delicately. It's my absolute belief that by not affording these kids the space and respect to be who they truly are, the system unwittingly sets them up for all sorts of problems in later life.*

## Mark

*It's strange that in the retelling of the story of Kiki's journey through school, I am now reminded of so many parallels between how Kiki struggled with school and how I struggled with school. Within the family, we often just assume that because I ended up doing well academically, the system must have somehow done its job. Well, academically, yes, the system did serve me well. But, when I reflect on the anxiety levels experienced by Kiki when it comes to teachers, being asked to answer questions, and the blind panic that goes with not knowing the answer, or more accurately, absolutely* knowing *the answer but being too afraid to even say it because the conditions of being asked and quizzed feel so intimidating . . . I realise in retrospect that I had just as much anxiety as Kiki going through the schooling system.*

*I can imagine many people saying, 'Well, why don't you just force her to go through the system and she too could end up (like you, Mark) highly qualified and academically successful?' The problem with this, for me, is that all these years later (and having now been a recovering alcoholic and addict for sixteen years) I learned from a very young age how to try and fix bad feelings with bad behaviour. I'm not saying I became an addict because I was scared to put my hand up in class at school – what I am saying is that the way in which I had absolutely no other choice but to keep ploughing forward, despite feeling fearful, led me to find unhealthy emotional 'solutions' in later life whenever I encountered stresses or fears. I genuinely believe the one-size-fits-all approach to education is directly responsible for what is often described as an epidemic of anxiety among our children.*

## Nadia

*All this pressure to be more extroverted had a very negative effect on Kiki. As I write this, I'm wondering what it might have felt like if at school my teacher had tried to encourage me to be shy rather than extrovert! I would have gone stark raving mad! When we picked her up from school, she would be so weary, and we could tell she had been crying. Every day. We would get home and, exhausted, she would flop onto the sofa, only for us to have to try and get her to the table to get the homework done! My instinct screaming to me yet again that there was something very wrong with what we were doing.*

*But we were now hurtling along a track in a runaway train we didn't even know we could get off.*

*I can honestly say that every bit of homework we did throughout their school life was a complete waste of time. It only ever served to confuse or stress the girls out, and us by extension. I've since discovered that any parent is allowed to inform their child's school that they don't want their child to do any homework at all. There is no law stating that a primary-school child has to do homework. If we had known this back then, we would have probably refused to do it. The same nagging thought kept creeping into my mind and heart, 'Surely, at the age of six, every kid should be playing, drawing, painting, dancing, watching cartoons, even rowing with her sister for the few hours before bedtime?' I never remember having any homework as an infant.*

## Mark

*On the subject of homework, I remember this being one of the areas that I began to sense that even a fee-paying school* such as ours wasn't entirely providing the exclusive experience we thought we were paying for. As a homeschooling parent, I have discovered subsequently that some of the printouts and worksheets that were sent home with Kiki and Maddie came from some readily available sources. We weren't getting access to unique or clever learning tools – these were bog-standard fodder printed out and sent home with our girls. Sometimes it wasn't even properly photocopied!

One of biggest red flags for me regarding how bad things were for Kiki, revolved around the school shows and assemblies. On a regular basis there would be readings, a violin demonstration, Harvest Festival, Easter Parade, etc. Events that required us parents to trot along and see our kids perform or sing. In years to come, I would bitterly refer to these fixtures as the school reassuring us parents that we were getting our money's worth. They were colourful, and they were a brilliant showcase for all the extroverted kids to jump up and sing their hearts out, stomping up and down proclaiming verse, feverishly playing their violins out of tune. For a shy child such as Kiki, they presented yet another horror to be endured.

On one particular occasion, I remember us sitting down and seeing immediately that Kiki had been crying. She was red-eyed – and while almost all the other kids were waving excitedly at their parents, Kiki couldn't look at us. Her hands in her mouth, she looked devastated.

Just writing this is very hard to do without getting as upset as we were upon seeing her. Somehow the performance ended – and afterwards Kiki broke down in tears, crying, desperately reaching her arms out to us as we went to leave. I remember looking at the teachers for help. They encouraged us to go – but everything about leaving her felt wrong. Everything. In retrospect, this was a defining moment. We weren't dealing with normal upset; this was something much, much deeper for Kiki. Driving in to work forty-five minutes later, I got a call telling me I would have to head back to the school and collect her. Kiki hadn't recovered – she'd got much, much worse.

The feeling that our daughter, through no real fault of the school (it was, after all, just doing what a prep school does – preparing children for a highly academic and competitive education and life) was essentially in an unsafe place (emotionally) felt very real.

But we didn't take action. Not yet.

It is no exaggeration to describe her as a deeply distressed child most mornings on her way to school. She would go silent. She would bite her lip. Her glasses would steam up. Tears would well up and drop.

One particularly vivid and lasting memory I have of Kiki at this age is me taking her to school most mornings and placing kisses in her pockets for the day ahead. The idea being, if she needed comfort, she could just reach into her pocket and get a kiss from me. Day by day, the number of kisses she wanted in her pockets would go up, to the point that, in the end, I was actively kissing my hand and placing it into her pocket a hundred times.

Only a year ago, while learning about something at the kitchen table, she said, 'Dad, you do know that I used every one of those kisses you put in my pockets?'

## Nadia

Red flags were popping up all the time, but we kept hoping we were wrong. I would dismiss doubts with, 'I'm over-reacting', 'I was shit at school, perhaps it's going to be the same for my kids'. 'All the other parents (surgeons, professors, doctors) are just so much better at all this "working parent" malarkey than me.' 'This is a very good private school. We're dishing out the dosh, they must be right, and I most definitely must be the one who is wrong.' It was hard not to keep returning to the thought, 'Poor Kiki, we've failed her terribly.'

There were many voices in my head and they were all pretty negative.

But she wasn't just an anxious child. Her problems seemed to revolve very specifically around school.

Whenever she'd get home after school and until we got the homework out of the way, she was always quite sad and tired. We'd then have approximately two hours before bed where she'd perk up, play with Maddie . . . and then just before bed she'd nosedive and get anxious and worried again about school.

At the weekends she would be fine from Friday afternoon

when we picked her up from school, through to late afternoon on Sunday when she would then get what I call 'Sunday-itis': a dread of the week to come, and start begging not to go to school again.

We finally got to what would have been Kiki's last year before moving up to the school for older children. I was getting more and more worried, as Kiki didn't seem to be improving in any of the subjects. It felt like she was just surviving, certainly not thriving. I remember Kiki saying to me one day, 'I'm not like the other children, Mum. I can't remember stuff. Why can't I?' How I wished I could give her an answer to this! We practiced things over and over again. She would understand exactly what we were doing but then the very next day she would have forgotten everything. I was getting desperate.

To be fair, the school shared their concerns about Kiki's problems with 'retention'. They started to mutter the words 'processing disorder'. I've since learnt from a teacher friend that, back then, even if they had suspected that Kiki had dyslexia, it was standard policy not to say anything unless the child was tested. Years later when we finally had her assessed by an educational psychologist, we discovered that this was in fact the case: she is dyslexic. Which was such a relief when we got the diagnosis. It explained so much. I wasn't mad. And, in fact, having learnt so much more about dyslexia, I'm pretty sure that I'm also dyslexic. I, like many others, had the complete misconception that everyone who has dyslexia has trouble reading. This is not the case. Kiki actually reads very well. Her dyslexia means she has a lot of trouble retaining what she's learnt, which is why we both still always joke about our terrible short-term memory!!

We had many meetings with the school and the Special Education Needs (SEN) teachers as they tried to assess what was going on for her. The teachers were worried about the fact that Kiki was finding it hard to retain what she was being taught. At that point, I wanted to take her for a full assessment with an educational psychologist, but the school were very against this. To their credit, they said she was too young and it could dent her confidence further. In fact, over the next few years, every time I looked into getting her assessed there were various reasons why it never happened. According to the school it can be quite an inexact science, with lots of false positives, plus Mark was always reluctant for Kiki to be tested because he felt it might label her in a negative way. I could totally understand and sympathise with Mark's view, but I was desperate to get an answer as to why she was struggling so much.

With hindsight, I think Mark was maybe struggling to come to terms with the fact that Kiki wasn't academic in the same way he was, and I sympathise with that. It's a big deal to shift your expectations. I, of course, didn't have the same feelings because I had never classed myself as being academic. I also don't think I've lost out because of it, either. In fact, I don't think I would have the life I love if I was more academically minded.

*Sometimes I wonder, if I had my time again, would I have liked to be tested for ADHD and dyslexia? And I think my answer would have to be no. I actually quite like my messed-up chaotic brain; and after all, who would I have been if they'd 'fixed' me?!*

*The school recommended that we took Kiki for a hearing test, which we did, even though I knew that was pointless – there was certainly nothing wrong with her hearing! If anything, her hearing was too good as she was very sensitive to noise, and this fact alone made life in the classroom very unpleasant for her. She had a particularly 'shouty' teacher and she would keep her hands over her ears to dull the volume. Whenever she flushed the toilet, she would put her hands over her ears straight away and run so she wouldn't have to hear the flush! Sadly, her struggles were not to do with her ears.*

*The teachers, trying to help once again, suggested that it might be a good idea to enrol her in Kumon (more on Kumon later) and private tutoring. On top of a full day of lessons and homework. We complied, even though my instinct was screaming at me that this was stark raving mad. Kiki was not able to retain what she was being taught at school. How on earth was trying to ram more stuff into her brain going to help? But my head, the peer pressure that I was perceiving thanks to my own insecurities surrounding my lack of a 'satisfactory' education, plus the guilt I felt about the fact that I was a working mum unable to attend to all the stuff other parents kept chatting about* in the playground, told me that if I didn't do as was recommended, our little girl would end up a complete failure. I was deciding her fate, contemplating her entire life – and she wasn't even SEVEN!

# Taking the plunge with Kiki

> We have sold ourselves into a fast-food model of education, and it's impoverishing our spirit and our energies as much as fast food is depleting our physical bodies.
>
> Sir Ken Robinson

The summer of 2013 was one of the worst summers of our lives.

Kiki was now hardly eating or sleeping, so her ability to remember anything was zero. Learning had given way to blind panic both for Kiki and us! We also found out that the teacher Kiki was scheduled to have in her next year was affectionately referred to as tough. Under normal circumstances, this is de rigueur in *any* school story. We all had teachers we didn't like, or teachers that didn't like us (and Maddie had gone through her fair share), but given Kiki's fragile state, this news was the straw that broke the camel's back.

We were beside ourselves. We all felt utterly trapped. What were we going to do? The local state schools had ever bigger classes and, given her shyness, we feared Kiki would have been eaten up and spat out. We couldn't even consider looking for a different private school as she was too far 'behind' to be accepted. She was only seven and we already felt like there were no options open to us!

It's important to stress that, at this particular point in time, Maddie was moving through the same school in what seemed like a totally satisfactory way. She seemed happy, she had close friends and was 'managing fine with her schoolwork', so all our energies naturally focused on resolving things as best as we could for Kiki.

Knowing how things would eventually play out for Maddie further down the line, when we reflect on this time, it is with sadness and regret that we realise we were choosing to assume all was fine with Maddie. On the surface it was. But then as we would all find out, Maddie is a fabulous performer! She could hide her emotions well.

## Nadia

*The day we discovered that homeschooling was even a possibility is etched on both of our memories. We had just come off the back of a Summer of Hell. The school that Kiki was attending had suggested we hot-housed her learning with Kumon lessons. For those who don't know, Kumon is a Japanese drill-teaching method, founded in 1958, to learn maths and English by doing worksheets every day and visiting a study centre twice a week. It was clearly implied that Kiki needed to pursue this extra-curricular activity (among others) in order to 'catch up' and reach the required levels for further 'progress'. The school had also suggested extra tutoring and had given us goals. For example, certain books to read which were beyond dry and boring, reading-age levels to aspire to, vocabulary lists to know off by heart (even if she didn't understand the words fully) and all to be completed over the summer holidays, a time when (in my opinion) a seven year old should be having fun. Again, although at the time we were deeply frustrated with the school, to be fair, they were just trying to get her to where she needed to be for an academic prep school.*

*Interestingly, four years later, when we had her assessed by an educational psychologist, she told us that none of these extra measures would have helped Kiki with her dyslexia. If anything, they could have just made it worse.*

*We had gone to Cornwall for our summer holidays and*

had rented a beautiful cottage with a pool overlooking the sea. An idyll - but I would wake up every morning with a feeling of absolute dread; the day stretching ahead, knowing that at some point I would have to pull Kiki away from the all the fun in the pool and try and shoehorn something, anything, from the pile of books I'd been given (by the school and her tutor) into her head. Almost every day that summer there would be a point where I would find myself looking for somewhere that I could have a little cry without being seen. I felt so sorry for Kiki and what we were putting her through. I had no doubt whatsoever that I had failed her terribly. Mark and I were getting more and more stressed with each other as we realised the enormity of the task. It was as if every morning we'd wake up and try and pour more water into a bucket with a hole at the bottom. The growing sense of doom was palpable.

The panic was all the more real because that coming September Kiki would be 'moving up' to the juniors, where the pressure would really pile on with SATs. We made a frantic call to her tutor to double her lessons as soon as we returned to London, in a bid to get her to where she needed to be academically. Mark joked that the number of exams, practise tests and papers were like her trying to gain qualifications and access to the bar! Again, my gut was telling me not to call the tutor and book extra lessons, but the societal and peer pressure on me to be at a certain stage in my parenting, and for Kiki to be at a certain age in her reading, numeracy, literacy, etc. were simply overwhelming. Constantly running alongside these academic worries were the more philosophical worries of, 'What if my daughter becomes a school-refuser?', 'What if this all means she will ultimately fail in life?', 'What if my daughter has a mental health crisis?'

## Mark

Every day we were having to go back over what we had done the day before, I felt more and more at sea not knowing how best to get the most basic of mathematical formulae into Kiki's head. After all, I wasn't a teacher, Nadia wasn't a teacher - that's what we pay the school to do, isn't it? It began to feel like she was simply phasing out; as if she had so bought into the idea of being a failure, that if anyone even asked her name she would pause, believing she might get the answer wrong. It was heart-breaking. Her self-esteem was at rock bottom and panic started to set in.

I realise in retrospect that I was getting increasingly angrier with the school. I couldn't understand why we were paying such enormous fees for Kiki to go to a school where the only guaranteed way for her to learn and make progress was by doing most of her learning outside the school. It didn't stack up for me. There was what felt like an enormous disconnect between the school talking about subjects and targets and thresholds while Kiki herself (despite all this outside help) was getting quieter and quieter and more and more anxious about going to school.

It was becoming more apparent that Kiki herself had a child's sense that things weren't going according to plan. Kids know when their parents are worried or stressing. No amount of concealing how we feel in words can hide the looks on our faces, or the tensions in our voices. If I really go back to that time and think of Kiki trying to make sense of things, it's still deeply upsetting. She was so confused and so stressed by a system that we - her parents - were, that summer, a huge part of. Although we knew she was in SEN (Special Educational Needs) classes, and yes, there may well be some form of dyslexia at work, it was palpable that most of the behaviour Kiki was demonstrating was more akin to extreme anxiety and stress.

Sitting on the cusp of Kiki's return to school, I was approaching tasks like a military drill. Because there were no alternatives (or so we thought), the best we could hope to do was essentially hold her hand back into school and into the minefield that would soon become SATs, reading ages and all the other barometers of success and failure. Without any clear alternatives, our only hope was to try to keep up morale, but the feeling that we were essentially getting her to walk the plank come school time was very real and worrying. As we sat, almost a week or so from going back to school, this was the point at which the very person the school had advised us to employ to support Kiki's learning uttered the words that would change all our lives forever.

## Nadia

I remember a couple of weeks before Kiki was due to go back to school, we bought her the most beautiful puppy. We had really gone to town with the whole surprise element, driving over 400 miles there and back to Cumbria to collect a tiny black and white cockapoo. Back at home, we blindfolded Kiki and all the family had gathered to watch the reveal. We were beyond excited, and as we lifted her blindfold and Chi Chi was put into her arms, it was a truly beautiful moment: tears, disbelief, the works. Everyone thought it was the cutest thing. But I was feeling something different. I was more worried than ever. The way Kiki broke down just seemed too extreme. She cried with joy. But then the crying just didn't stop. And within the same breath of having fallen in love with her puppy, she told me later she was worrying about going back to school. It was like all the fear, worry and anxiety she'd been hiding had poured out and onto her new puppy.

A week after 'Puppygate', we were both downstairs while Kiki was having a lesson upstairs with her tutor. At the end of the lesson, her tutor asked to talk with us. My heart dropped as I remember feeling so fearful she was going to tell us something terrible.

It's such a vivid memory, Mark and I walking into the room, seeing Kiki's tutor with a very serious face. We let Kiki go to her room, and her tutor went on to say, 'I really do think Kiki will struggle this coming year [she was an ex teacher at Kiki's school] – I think it could possibly leave her very unhappy'. Then she asked the killer question: 'Have you heard of homeschooling?'

I immediately said something like, 'Homeschooling? What the HELL is that?' I had a rush of excitement! I looked at Mark wide-eyed! Could we have an answer to our prayers? Although this was exactly what I needed to hear, running directly parallel to this excitement was the knowledge that a qualified teacher had just told us that Kiki may very well be unable to handle carrying on at school. Joy was accompanied by dismay. Here was another confirmation that we had failed her. As it was for Mark, the fear of failure was now a different sort of failure. We didn't want her to fail within the system, but were we about to set ourselves up for an even bigger failure by stepping outside of it?

As we've described, Mark and I came from very different educational backgrounds. While for me, the idea of pulling the girls out of conventional schooling was undeniably radical, it didn't feel fraught with danger in the way it did for Mark. Although I had huge fear, and yes it felt extraordinarily scary, it also felt very brave too. I had faith (albeit blind faith) that we could pull this off!

I suppose having gone through life with nothing more than one O Level, I felt there could be an alternative way through. Mark, I think it's fair to say, had more skin in the game when it came to academic qualifications and how they directly helped him in his life. So, in very different ways, as we sat on the cusp of taking one of our girls out of mainstream *education, you could probably say we were both very much on the same page, we were just . . . using different pens!*

*As soon as the tutor left, we searched online and discovered quite quickly that all we had to do was contact the council and deregister her. Just like that! It was like the heavens had opened and all the angels were singing.*

## Mark

*Although I definitely experienced something akin to a heavenly visitation, I also felt as though the levies were about to burst and we were about to be overwhelmed. As the words 'Have you ever considered homeschooling?' ricocheted around my mind, I couldn't help but start to project all those countless potential narratives of a homeschooled kid. Many of the images described at the beginning of this book passed before my eyes. I knew (for a fact) we needed a swift and immediate solution to stop the upset - but this?! Really? Everything went into slow motion - and while we started the process of removing her from school, I truly worried that we could be consigning Kiki to academic Armageddon!*

*I wrote a quick letter by email to the head of Kiki's school. We contacted the council and requested to meet. Kiki meanwhile was visibly deflated. All tension was already flooding from her, and so tears of fear were quickly replaced with tears of joy, relief and probably disbelief that this was even happening. From what we could gather, there appeared to be no requirement to follow the curriculum, no inspections, no checks, no suggestions that we were weird or strange or wrong. It was simple. To be honest, we were all in total shock. You have to apply in triplicate to take your kid out of school to go on holiday during term time, and yet here we were, allowed to take our child out of school immediately, no questions asked. Could this really be the answer? Could we have a happy child again? We knew we'd done something right for sure. But there was also a huge sense of failure. How much had Kiki's school experience broken her spirit? What lasting damage could we have inflicted already? And were we about to fuck it all up again in an even bigger way?!*

## Nadia

*I will never forget the look on Kiki's face when we told her she wouldn't be going back to school. I thought I'd understood just how unhappy she had been. But when I saw her crumple up with relief, I realised that her feelings had run deeper than we'd feared. I knew in that moment that we were absolutely doing the right thing. I was elated. I could now right all the wrongs I believed I'd done. I could assuage my guilt. Maybe, I could even get back the happy child I had had before she went to school. I was in the pink cloud of discovering that I had a choice. The sense of relief was palpable.*

*A week later and I'm shitting myself. Mark was panicking.*

*His mum thought we had taken leave of our senses, and we were banned from telling his grandmother for fear of granny reprisals! Bless him, Mark was a product of a very good traditional education and had always imagined that all his girls would follow the same path. He was now reeling. And I, who had skived and bunked off throughout my education, had no idea where to start or what to do.*

*Luckily, my mum and dad were a hundred per cent behind our decision to take Kiki out of school. And coincidentally they just happened to have a friend whose daughter had been homeschooling her two sons for years. This was a godsend. We met up with them within days and talked for hours. Mark and I were desperate to know where to start. And I can honestly say we took every bit of her advice. I will always be eternally grateful to her for pointing us in the right direction. And in fact, over the years, I have passed my contact details on to many parents who have reached out, desperate for help in those first bewildering days of taking their children out of the system and swimming against the tide. She put me in touch with various homeschooling groups in our area, which were to become a real lifeline of support and eventually give us so much advice.*

## Mark

*Although I had an academic 'shit-show' playing in the back of my mind, I do remember the moment of taking Kiki out* of school as one of huge relief. A HUGE relief. When you're seeing your child suffer from what look like the symptoms of depression and extreme anxiety, you're willing to embrace whatever options there are that might alleviate the distress. For the short term, it felt like we had pulled Kiki to safety. But as is the way with all these sorts of decisions in a family, there was the distant beating drum of worry surrounding Maddie.

At this point in time, she appeared to be moving through the same school with no obvious signs of stress or worry, but we were increasingly aware that she was languishing in some of the lower sets, and was potentially moving through the school 'under the radar' and 'under-achieving', but still no one was really telling us we needed to change anything in our approach to her learning.

However, if Nadia and I are truly honest with ourselves and each other, we were both also extremely busy with work around this time, and where we felt we could, we were relying on that original thought that drove us toward private school in the first place: 'We are paying the school a lot of money, surely the school will pick up the slack with Maddie.' After all – she was a much more confident kid.

For now, though, Kiki was 'safe'. But now, the questions and expressions of doubt started coming. My grandmother and my mother viewed her removal from formal school as some kind of a strange hippy weirdness. Was this really the right thing to do? Isn't a huge part of school all about working things out? What will she do about GCSEs? Will she take her GCSEs? What about socialising? How are you going to balance this with your working lives? What about Maddie?

This was one of the more surprising discoveries about deciding to take Kiki out of school. The extent to which members of my extended family doubted our decision. They knew we were trying to do right for Kiki, but they had real concerns about whether turning our back on conventional schooling altogether was really the right move. In retrospect, I realise these were all reasonable and rational questions to ask, but I remember feeling very tetchy and snappy about them. Firstly, no one fully realised what a state of emergency we felt we were in. Kiki was a quiet and shy kid and so she only ever really opened up about things to her mum. Secondly, things were moving so fast that, to be brutally honest, we didn't yet have the answers to any of these questions ourselves.

We hadn't made the decision based on any ideology or school of thought. We weren't doing it as an anarchic act of sticking our middle finger up to the establishment. It was a needs must situation. It wasn't even as if we had read all the literature (and as we found out, there's not an awful lot), and we certainly hadn't yet become Ken Robinson groupies.

All I do remember thinking and feeling was giddy and disorientated about the palpable lack of answerability to the local authorities. To this day it still surprises me how easy it is to take full control of your child's education.

## Nadia

*While Mark kept wittering on about the 'astonishing legality of it all', I discovered quite quickly that there was a fair amount of disagreement among other homeschooling parents about how cooperative you should be, or needed to be, with your local authority. While it's really important to stress that it's entirely legal to take your child out of school, I met a lot of parents who were very wary about the authorities – understandably so, as there were stories of some local authorities overstepping the mark.*

*I would often have the United Nations quoted to me: 'The respect of parent's freedom to educate their children according to their vision of what education should be has been part of international human rights standards since their emergence', and it was reiterated time and again that as parents we have a God-given right to educate our children as we see fit. Every child has a right to be educated, just not necessarily in a school. This idea was delicious to me. I had absolutely no idea that we could have such autonomy over our children's education.*

*I have to say that we were truly blessed with our particular local authority and the liaison officer we were automatically assigned, but this isn't the case for all homeschooling parents and many people's experiences aren't always positive. The general consensus ran, that although it wasn't illegal to homeschool, some authorities would nevertheless try to gently enforce the mainstream system of* learning (subjects, syllabuses, GCSEs and A Levels, etc.) by stealth; so I came across a lot of understandable nervousness, suspicion and a general reluctance to even engage.

## Mark

I must admit, I very much allowed the fact that many home-schooling parents were suspicious of the local authorities to fuel my own admittedly jaundiced, prejudiced and stereotypical ideas that we were on the cusp of entering a community not too dissimilar from some kind of Moonie cult. My take on things was that if we aren't doing anything illegal, what have we got to hide? At this stage of the proceedings, I was very against the idea of Kiki continuing in her school - but if I'm honest, I was hoping this was only going to be a temporary solution. I certainly wasn't anti 'the system'. Not yet, anyway!

I felt terribly at sea. I was worried that in a matter of weeks, Nadia was going to be asking me to join her and other hippy parents to sit in circles around fires, playing guitars, smoking spliffs, discussing the merits of certain natural herbal remedies for lice infestations. Looking back, the fear of not fitting into this new culture was as real as the inability to fit into the Yummy Mummy Social Olympics that had been occurring at the school gates every morning for the past however many years.

Why were these homeschoolers all so anti the local

*authorities? What were they hiding? Why were they so sensitive? Were we about to consign our daughter to a world of anarchic rule-breakers all smelling of patchouli oil?!*

## Nadia

*The first time I met up with any homeschooling parents was at a homeschool park group. I'm not sure who was more nervous, Kiki or me. We certainly held each other's hands very tightly! It was a bit like a mother and baby group for older children, with all the parents drinking coffee and munching packed lunches, talking nineteen to the dozen while watching their kids hurl themselves about on rope swings.*

*It's quite rare to ever 'drop off' your kids in the homeschool world. Kiki was ecstatic as she realised I wasn't handing her over to anyone; I would be in the vicinity the entire time. While she was relieved, by contrast I felt like I stuck out like a sore thumb – a highly strung, super anxious sore thumb. In fact, I'm sure I must have looked to them like the other private-school parents had looked to me, back when I was failing miserably as a 'perfect prep school parent': neurotic, on edge, worried about getting everything right and stressed. Because I'm quite a proud person, I probably wasn't looking quite like I felt, which was a wee bit desperate and scared.*

*All I remember thinking was, would I ever find a mum tribe that I would feel comfortable with?!*

*Everyone I spoke to that day recommended exactly what*

we'd heard from countless other quarters: watch this man called Sir Ken Robinson's Ted Talk on how schools kill creativity. Sir Ken Robinson is a maverick educational advisor to the government, with a specialised focus on the arts, and a turn of phrase that captured both mine and Mark's imaginations.

He immediately became our secret crush. It felt like he had got inside our heads and articulated exactly what we needed to hear, or maybe what in our heart of hearts we always knew to be true, but assumed was absolutely mad of us to think or entertain.

## Mark

And so . . . we watched Ken Robinson's Ted Talk . . .

Very . . . very . . . slowly . . . I felt my anxiety beginning to subside . . . This man and his ideas had a huge impact on us. He also allowed me to (rather sniffily and arrogantly) consider that even highly educated people could feel disillusioned with the mainstream educational system. It was, without exaggeration, a turning point for us both.

Ken Robinson's basic theory is that creativity is driven out of us from a young age due to an education system that is predicated on equipping and educating young minds in the way that best suits the economic needs of society. Of course, he believes in the importance of literacy and numeracy but, as he states, 'creativity is every bit as important as literacy'.

*Throughout his very funny and very engaging talk, he expresses concern about an educational system that in no way caters for difference, that increasingly marginalises creativity, and misses out on the specialness of learning. He invokes Picasso, 'All children are born artists, the problem is remaining one as we grow up', and given that we were a family obsessed with and defined by the arts, this concept spoke to me.*

*Questions were ricocheting around my head. What is education about? Learning things in order to become a vital cog in someone else's wheel of life, or expanding your mind and soul so that you can better decide for yourself what your life is? Should education only be about remembering stuff without truly feeling what it all means? Quite quickly the tug of war between conventional education and homeschooling became an intellectual tug of war between these two thoughts. As I was fretting and worrying philosophically . . . Nadia first introduced the expression* radical de-schooling! *I'm not exaggerating when I say I came out in a huge rash as she started to explain to me what she thought was going to be best for Kiki.*

## Nadia

*Next we read John Holt's book* How to Homeschool Your Children. *A lot of it is a bit outdated now, but his basic philosophy got me really excited as I felt I had something to* pin what we were planning onto. Reading his book gave me a little confidence that with trust and patience we would be able to 'facilitate' Kiki's learning in an exciting, gentle way. But first we were going to have to go through something pretty scary!

John Holt, and almost every homeschooler I've ever met, advocates a period of de-schooling for any child moving from the school system to homeschooling. This basically means for every year a child has been at school, you give them a whole month of total freedom, where they choose exactly how they spend their day with no formal learning at all.

This works as an adjustment period for them to transition from formal learning to child-led learning. The belief being that for a child to really get the benefits of homeschooling, they have to decompress and disconnect from the effects of 'school ways' and find a new normal. Of course, the parent has to, too, and for Mark and me that was a bigger challenge than we bargained for!

We really had to hold our nerve because, as the daughter of my parent's friends said, it wasn't only Kiki who was shell-shocked by what she had gone through at school; we were too.

We had become institutionalised into thinking that every minute of our child's life had to be taken up with being 'busy'. It's hard when you have spent so much time fire-fighting, pushing, cajoling and encouraging, to suddenly stand back, lift your hands up and say, 'Take your time, find what makes your heart sing.'

That is effectively what de-schooling is all about. Kiki had no idea what made her heart sing, she didn't know how to self-start anything because she hadn't been given the space to. Even weekends (a time you'd be forgiven for thinking was meant for family and playtime) had been spent doing extra homework and tutor sessions with us desperately trying to push things into her brain – a brain that was eventually so befuddled it had zero desire to take anything in.

Sundays were a write-off, too, because her anxiety about Monday morning and the return to school would be off the scale. Thank God for art galleries and cinema, as those little outings were the only real times of respite. Later, we will talk about how cinema and art became the centre of everything for Kiki. A happy ending is on the horizon folks!

## Mark

The decision to de-school sat very uncomfortably with me. In the middle of work, I'd get a giddy sort of vertigo feeling – as if I was looking down from a great height, while looking up at an utterly unscalable summit. I very much felt that my job at this time was to present a confident and decisive front to all those family members and friends who were arching their eyebrows or gasping with surprise. While in the boiler room (so to speak) Nadia was starting to help Kiki come back down to earth from a place of high anxiety.

*I knew that Kiki needed some time to settle, but I'd be lying if I didn't say I had grave doubts about our decision from an educational perspective. De-schooling sounded very hippy to me; and yet I knew we had to take our foot off the pedal with Kiki. I spent most of my time looking online for textbooks and online learning tools that would best approximate the learning she would have received at school, but whenever I wanted to talk about these things Nadia would repeat her refrain, 'She is de-schooling.' I did the maths – she'd been at school for approximately four to five years – so de-schooling was going to be almost half a year . . . HALF A YEAR?!?!?*

*I suspect that my state of mind at this time was very similar to that of every parent the length and breadth of the country when the coronavirus pandemic landed. Horrified parents faced with wide-eyed kids sitting at dining tables or on sofas looking back at them. Is it safe to de-school?! Will it be lost time? How were we going to teach her? I was well educated, I'd done some lecturing at art colleges and film schools, but I had never sat with a child and tried to teach them about number bonds or fractions. I realised almost immediately how reliant I was on the education system to sort everything out for us. It was as though a life support had suddenly been removed. Having been sober for sixteen years now, I can only describe the worry and fear I was feeling at the time in terms of an addiction. I was co-dependent on the system – and without it, I was fearful I could go cold turkey!*

## A top tip for all parents facing a similar situation

STOP. Take a deep breath and stay calm. No amount of worrying or panicking is going to make the situation better. It will only make it worse, and your child will undoubtedly pick up on your stress. For the new homeschooling parent, it's critically important to remind yourself that you *do* have time on your side; and you *do* have the law on your side. It's absolutely fine to hunker down and allow yourself time to adjust to this 'new normal' – to coin a phrase!

Contrary to what the experts and educationalists have been saying in lockdown recently, taking a little bit of time to recalibrate your child's education is *not* going to condemn them to the slag heap of learning. That said, it *is* very hard to hold your nerve when all around you exams are being taken, SATs being assessed, and numeracy and literacy targets being hit.

Remember, if you've taken *your* child out of mainstream schooling out of necessity or choice, stay *firm* and ignore the nay-sayers and doubters. You are about to take *more* responsibility for your child's learning, not less.

It's much more challenging to be microscopically

responsible for *every* part of your child's education rather than essentially handing all (or most) of the responsibility over to a school – and *remember*, it isn't written on a tablet of stone somewhere that learning has to happen only between the hours of 8.50 a.m. (just before assembly) and 3.30 p.m. (home time)!

# Every child is different

## Our experience with Maddie

> For most of us, the problem isn't that we aim too high and fail. It's just the opposite: we aim too low and succeed.
>
> Sir Ken Robinson

Although Kiki was the first of our girls to be home-schooled, our eldest daughter Maddie had a very different and, in many ways, bumpier journey towards home-schooling.

Whereas there was a sense of impending disaster at quite an early stage for Kiki-Bee (due to her age, her eye, her anxiety) Maddie was more adept at socially cruising through the demands of prep school. She had a much happier journey through nursery, reception and infant school . . . But, where things started to get tricky was as Maddie (alongside all her classmates) started to move inexorably on an ever-accelerating conveyor belt towards the academic assessments and exams that would dictate which school she would 'be able' to go to aged eleven.

An entirely new horror story was about to unfold before our eyes.

## Nadia

*If you were to ask Maddie, she would say she was happy enough at school until year 6. Up until then she had a couple of good friends, she liked her teachers, her teachers liked her. She had a bit of a reputation for talking more than listening in class (who does that sound like?), but she was happy. She would frequently get awards for being kind while other kids got awards for maths or science or English. In retrospect, we should have sensed something of an academic pinch-point coming down the line. But, by and large, she genuinely liked school.*

*However, when she arrived at year 6, it was like hitting a brick wall. Suddenly it was all about taking tests, sitting mock exams, studying past examination papers and cribbing the kinds of questions asked for entrance exams. It was a bit soul-destroying for her, because she found the whole testing experience so difficult. So many more children than we like to think, or the system dares to admit, are like this. If I had one huge wish with the educational system as it is, it would be that 'test fear' would be taken more seriously.*

## Mark

*I often liken having more than one child to standing in the middle of a battlefield and being attacked from all sides. My eldest daughters Issy and Fleur were somewhat blessed, in that a state secondary and a grammar school did the required job for them both. My direct involvement, as an absent parent, was diluted, but they were always happy pushing through their schools. They had their fair number of issues with friends, but they both took to the educations they received. Their challenges were different; their mum and dad weren't together, they travelled between two homes, they had two younger sisters pop into their lives.*

*With Maddie and Kiki, over the years it's very much felt like as soon as one child's problem is resolved, a new crisis erupts for the other one. And so it was with Maddie.*

*Just as we felt we had hit on a solution for Kiki, Maddie's education within the private fee-paying system suddenly came into very sharp focus. I became increasingly concerned as the disconnect was beginning to reveal itself between the work Maddie was being sent home with to revise and prepare for, and her ability to complete it. She was bright . . . but she* was struggling to get the required marks that would give her the right 'scores' or 'numbers' to qualify for the entrance exams of this or that school. She was suddenly being sent home with past entrance-exam papers almost every day. The aim was to essentially keep practising and practising until her scores improved to the right level.

With Kiki now experiencing 'learning liberation', the contrast between the two girls' experiences couldn't have been more stark. With every new entrance exam paper sent home I increasingly wondered, 'Is the measure of a child's intelligence or comprehension really best served by a one hour "memory" test?'

I'm not exaggerating when I say that as Maddie got closer and closer to the end of year 6, I felt like I was trying to control a careening car as it became involved in a slow-motion pile up. The workload (at home) was steadily increasing, but we weren't being given any tools to help her by the school. I remember the parents' evenings being an absolute sham. We would be ushered into a hall. There would be someone standing with a bell, and we were allowed to sit with each teacher for no longer than two minutes before the bell was rung. Nothing substantive was ever talked about, and every time I asked the school directly about whether she was 'on target' or 'keeping up with their expectations of her', I would be told that she was 'doing just fine'. Naturally this resulted in us thinking that, okay, she obviously really needs all this outside help (tutors and Kumon, etc.), and the school definitely seems to think it's all helping.

It was beginning to appear as though by sending your child to a fee-paying private school, that the school can never be seen to acknowledge an insufficiency in the education of your child . . . they have to be seen to be giving you value for money. It felt like the unwritten rule here was that you were supposed to spend yet more money employing an army of private tutors to help cram more and more information into your kids' heads, outside formal schooling, in order to get them to the levels required.

OR - and this may well have been too crushing a thing to realise and admit at the time ( as a biased and loving parent) - maybe, just maybe, when it came to this highly academic and competitive preparatory school, were we actually trying to squeeze a square peg (Maddie) into a round hole? Looking back, although I feel there was a lot wrong with the way Maddie was 'lost' in the system, I do also view this time as perhaps one of parental denial. We were naive. If the school said she was fine - we trusted them, and continued to believe that by paying all this money we could somehow buy her an education.

It's taken many years since to accept that we had chosen the wrong type of school for our daughter, but I do think the school itself showed little manoeuvrability when it came to doing what was actually needed to help Maddie succeed in their system. We were caught in the headlights of trying to get Maddie through just three to six months of school, ready for some of the most competitive senior schools in South London. We were panic-stricken.

## Nadia

*Those months were horrendous. Maddie was getting more and more despondent. She kept getting low marks. The more she 'failed', the more she panicked. The more everyone tried to pretend she hadn't 'failed', the more she knew we were all bullshitting her. And that's the thing about kids. We all like to think we can hide things from them. But if they are struggling in class, they know they're struggling. Maddie was well aware (as we have since discovered) that she was behind the rest of the class. We knew that Maddie was a bright kid. Her problem was that she struggled under test conditions. We knew things weren't good when she came home from school one day and asked us, 'What do I do if I don't get into any of the posh schools?' Apparently, all the kids had been running around comparing grades, showing off about this or that hugely impressive school they were going to, and comparing percentages from their test entrance exams.*

*There was a distinct sense of impending doom, or as Mark described it, it was like a runaway train.*

*One day, in the midst of Maddie's interviews and open days (God, how I hated those open days!!) for all of these ludicrously academic schools, I was hanging out with her at the weekend and I asked in a silly voice, 'So, Barly McGrew, How are YOU?'*

*There I was expecting us to giggle and chat about something fairly benign, only to get the shock of my life when her immediate answer was, 'Do you mean about school?'*

'No,' I replied, 'about YOU. Why, what's wrong with school?'

At which point she slid down the wall with huge, silent tears rolling down her face. 'Mum, I know I'm a failure,' she said, 'but DON'T WORRY - I've accepted I will never be good at anything . . .'

I was so shocked. I could not believe that any child of mine would say such a thing. I had no idea that this was how she had been thinking or feeling. It was so contrary to what I was picking up from her emotionally. How could I have not known this?? Parental guilt coursed through my veins yet again.

Recently, we were talking about this time, and Maddie confirmed that, 'Yes, I just accepted I was stupid - all of us who weren't in the top group felt we were stupid.' She added, 'It felt like the teachers only ever really made any effort with those kids in the bottom group who had the potential to get out of the bottom group. The rest of us were left behind.' To this day I can still be taken straight back to the anxiety and stress of that time whenever Maddie talks about her experiences.

## Mark

When Nadia told me this, I couldn't contain myself. My immediate desire was to nuke the school. I needed to let off steam somehow, I probably ran on a treadmill like a nutter for hours. Back then I was very much clouded with a sense of injustice. How on earth could a child of ours feel a failure at the age of ten? What the hell has gone wrong here? What part of paying for a private school to educate our daughter to the right level didn't make sense? What happened to concentrating on the struggling students to bring them up to the level of the successful students? What I didn't realise yet (which would come to me outside the system) was that this school had essentially done nothing wrong. The only people who had done anything wrong were us in sending them there!

It became increasingly apparent to us that the fee-paying school system is precisely what it says on the tin: a business, a money-making device just like every other form of money-making venture. The school maintained its academic prowess and reputation by maintaining its high number of academic success stories . . . which is fine if your kid is an academic success – but the system didn't and wasn't working given the situation we found ourselves in. Maddie probably wasn't going to do as well as she would need to in entrance exams . . . we were heading towards the end of the conveyor belt . . . and I could see trouble heading our way. Yes, I took her to open days at various schools, but when I think back to these trips and the interviews she did with the teachers – I come out in hives recalling how much I was willing things to be fine, while deep down knowing I was trying to force my dear daughter into a school uniform and a way of school life that just wasn't right for her.

By now, red flags were being raised everywhere. We met with the headmaster and what he had to say was that her scores were too low to go to the schools some of her friends were going to. I became panic-stricken that unless we did something quick, Maddie was about to fall through a major trapdoor, a trapdoor that could well dent her confidence, her self-esteem and her self-belief forever.

With the benefit of hindsight, I see myself at this time as something of a headless chicken, in complete denial about the fact that our daughter was not right for this school, the school was not right for our daughter, and that the system we had unwittingly (and with every good intention) placed her into, simply wasn't right for her. It's hard to admit, even now, that so much of what was going on for me (more than it was, in many ways, for Nadia) was a reluctance to accept that a lot of what I was feeling was about my expectations as a father, rather than anything to do with Maddie herself. Her private school journey, like Kiki's, wasn't meant to be. How much of this was me having to come to terms with the fact that things hadn't and weren't going the way I wanted them to? How much of all this was my fault for trying to give them both the school experience I had always wanted for myself? Moments of realisation like this rarely get easier, but I hope they can function as a stark warning to others. I did struggle with the idea of them not being super academic. Nadia, by contrast, didn't have this fear, because she hadn't had this dream for them in the first place

## Nadia

*My aim for the girls was that a private school would let them be whatever they truly were – regardless of how academic they were or could be. Although it might sound naive, when I sent them to a preparatory school, I thought it was going to prepare them for life in general, rather than prepare them for a very specific route through life in terms of their careers and learning. It actually came as something of a surprise when this particular narrative didn't come true. It was very clear Maddie didn't fit the system, and it was clear that any child struggling wouldn't deliver for the school stats. I vividly remember Mark and I meeting with the headmaster; he didn't know her like we did, she was simply a set of numbers in a spreadsheet. In retrospect, I even have a feeling that if I had challenged him to, he wouldn't have been able to put her face to her name let alone the numbers. He talked about where she was 'lacking', where she was 'low', what she would need to get into this second-to-last school choice. It was horrible. I remember stumbling out of his office and sitting in the car with Mark with a distinct sense of feeling trapped. On one level I realised we hadn't had our finger on the pulse with Maddie. I realised that whenever they had said she was 'fine' it suited us to think she was fine, when clearly, she wasn't. In many ways, perhaps the simple act of paying for school had been used by us both as a way to stave off guilt, giving us a false sense of security.*

*In fact, every bloody time we went in to see the headmaster*

*I invariably came out feeling upset and as though I'd somehow failed Maddie. Mark would try comforting and placating me on the way out but it always cut very deep. It felt like there was something more that we needed to be doing, that we were all having to jump over higher and higher hurdles. So, like Kiki, on the school's recommendation Maddie started to do Kumon. This involved half an hour of extra maths and half an hour of extra English at home every day of the week. Maddie's only dry observation being, 'I now know why the logo is of a kid's miserable face', and we reluctantly found a tutor to help with Maddie's maths.*

*If friends ever asked, 'Why don't you just send her to a state school?' it just didn't feel like an option as far as we were concerned. The state schools in our area at the time were terrible, we couldn't move to a new house, and even if we had sent her, our real fear was that Maddie would have seen herself as a categoric failure. She was in many ways so far into the system she had to find a completely alternative way out of it that wouldn't be seen as a 'step down' in her peer group. Once again, like Mark says, how much of this would she have felt, and how much of it was simply the way we felt? We may never know the full truth on this one.*

*What we did know, however, without a shadow of a doubt was that Maddie absolutely came to life when she was dancing, singing and performing. Almost every night she would choreograph dance routines to film music Mark would dig out for her. She went to Stagecoach at the weekends and* thrived, whether she was in a lead role or bossing other kids around on stage to stand in the right places. She was obsessed with the lyrics of every song we ever listened to - demanding Mark give her the CD cases to sing along. She was a fervent filmgoer. Everything that made her heart sing was anathema to the highly academic demands and needs of the school she was in.

## Mark

I remember once asking Maddie about the conversations with other kids at her school and she would always remark on the fact that if she mentioned a film, a TV show, a theatre show or even an exhibition she'd been to, she would always be met with not just silence, but a bemused and blank expression, like she was talking a completely different language. Where she wanted to talk about actors and filmmakers or even painters, she'd be met with a preference for maths equations or science experiments. Indeed, she said recently that the brighter kids at school would run around the playground teasing the kids in lower sets with trick questions about the time and maths as a means of gameplay. Such a shame she didn't have the confidence to do the same with names of actors, artists and directors!!

I remember her saying that the other kids in her class were only ever doing 'other' lessons outside of school. They never went to see films or look at art . . . and so she found herself having little in common with the kids around her. Details like this would raise yet more little red flags.

Now don't get us wrong, We all know most kids prefer the arts to the 'difficult' stuff on the syllabus – but when I look back I genuinely feel that our decision to send her to a school that only really valued the academic (with all the arts being of secondary importance) is a mistake we may well regret for the rest of our lives. Not because we eventually found a way out with homeschooling, but because somewhere inside Maddie's mind, the entire experience had (and I sometimes worry still has) convinced her that she 'wasn't academic' or 'intellectual'.

Given what we've learnt on our homeschooling odyssey ever since, the idea that Maddie could have ever considered herself to be unintelligent is quite distressing. Indeed, I've spent most of my married life insisting that despite Nadia's lack of formal qualifications, I have never known or met anyone as emotionally and instinctively intelligent as her. The markers of intellect aren't just academic.

It was around this time that my own attitude towards learning started to come under scrutiny as a consequence of the mistakes we had made. What is intelligence? What about emotional intelligence? Creative intelligence? Are you bright only when you can solve complex algebraic formulas? Do you have a grasp of history only if you can remember dates and times? For the first time, I was face to face with the idea that this daughter we had who was creative and interested in experiential things, just wasn't good at maths and wasn't good at English in a test environment. What on earth could we do about this? Well, given that her prep school had her heading towards entrance exams like a runaway train, there was only one thing we felt we could do with Maddie. Jump off the train!

## Nadia

Our first homeschooling decision was to hit the brakes and change Maddie's educative direction by focusing on what really made her heart sing. Music, dance, singing, and acting! The next move felt like a no-brainer. Let's rescue her from the fee-paying experience of academic Armageddon, and instead try a fee-paying stage school where she could indulge in her every passion. Within a matter of days, she had an audition set up for her at a top stage school. Bless her, she was only ten, but she had to sing, dance and act in front of a panel of judges and take a full written exam all on the same day. Remember, her self-esteem was on the floor, and here she was trying to pirouette her way into a new school as well as getting maths questions right! She must have been punch-drunk with confusion. And yet, she rose to the challenge, and joy of joys she was offered a place. We were all elated. We felt that we had found the solution, and that at least on one front we had things slightly more under control. How wrong could we have been?

# First year of homeschooling

## Getting to know our child and de-schooling with Kiki

> *Creativity is as important as literacy.*
> Sir Ken Robinson

When it comes to giving practical advice that you can enact almost immediately, we would suggest that it's critical to know what your kids are passionate about first and then trace back from this to identify what types of learning will best feed into it. This may sound frustratingly simple to say (it is!), but it's actually very tricky to do. Weirdly, most parents like to feel that they *already* know who their children are. It's one of the big mistakes we often make as parents. We view our children through that most wonky of lenses - *ourselves*. Most parents, although reluctant to admit it, only ever really judge their children in terms of how they compare to themselves and their own learning experiences.

Whether we have liked it or not, over the years Maddie has always veered towards the performing arts and Kiki towards the visual arts. We've tried to put all other types of subjects and learning experiences in front of them, but they have always ended up gravitating back towards these creative zones.

One of the biggest myths around homeschooling is that, as a parent, you are somehow going to renege on your responsibilities to equip your child with the bare essentials - numeracy and literacy. Nothing could be further from the truth. It may well be more challenging to keep them up to speed in these areas when compared to the rapid progress required by the national curriculum, but every homeschooler recognises the importance of literacy and numeracy - they just believe in getting there via a different route.

What is clear, however, is that our entire cultural attitude to learning and education is based around the belief that the creative subjects (or the humanities) are in some way softer, easier or less rigorously academic than, say, the sciences, maths and technologies. There is a hierarchy of subjects, and more often than not the creative arts, while seen as a good 'outlet' for our kids, are not treated seriously in the same way. This is where our attitudes to learning began to chime significantly with the ideas of Sir Ken Robinson.

At its simplest, if you can find that original burning creative light of joy in your child, and if you harness it correctly, you can turn it to countless other ends. In his essay *On Listening*, Plutarch wrote, 'The mind is not a vessel to be filled but a fire to be kindled.' And Einstein claimed, 'I never teach my pupils, I only attempt to provide the conditions in which they can learn.'

What is it that makes *your* child unique? Of course, we are *not* saying all children must be artists, we are simply saying we should try to understand what makes our children creatively happy and start from there. For instance, Maddie was forever drawn to nature, and one of our regrets is that she might have moved in different directions if we hadn't lived in Central London and could have indulged her passion for wildlife more.

### What makes their hearts sing?

All of parenting is about making difficult choices, but one absolute truism is that 'getting to know what truly makes your child's heart sing' is the single best piece of advice if you are deciding to change the course of your child's learning in any way.

Every passion or hobby has the potential to become the origin story of a later-chosen course of study (or even a career). A love of films – film studies – working in film or TV; a love of fashion – textiles and design; a love of big buildings or machines – engineering, architecture or surveying; a love of console games – coding; a love of complicated stories and politics – law, etc.

So, our advice from the outset is: get to know your kids in whatever way possible. Become expert in their passions, become a keen observer of what makes their hearts sing, immerse yourself in the things that excite them. Once you know their passions in more detail (in a 360-degrees way), you'll feel more equipped to then explore this passion in countless different ways through various other subjects and novel approaches.

If done correctly, de-schooling can be the first step in the right direction to getting to know your child on a much deeper more meaningful level.

On a practical level, of course we knew they would *have* to cover certain educational fundamentals such as maths and English on their homeschooling odyssey, but now there were going to be zero rules and regulations as to how we should or could achieve this. Yes, you've guessed it, creativity can *even* be the *key* to making strides in numeracy and literacy.

More refreshing still, was the fact that we also knew we could place far more emphasis on those subjects they loved (art, music, English literature and film) while finding creative ways to deliver other key subjects such as history, geography and PE, etc. We also knew that we would be able to find time to teach them, or let them rub up against, completely new subjects that are given virtually no emphasis in most schools, such as cooking, filmmaking and politics.

## Nadia

*AHHHH! De-schooling . . . All the home-ed mums I spoke to encouraged me to really relish this part of the process. By all accounts this was the moment you got your child back. You reconnected. It was going to be like 're-growing the umbilical cord'. Don't get me wrong, I'm much more of a hippy than Mark, and I swear by a holistic approach to the body and the mind – but even I got a bit wobbly about the next step. We didn't realise it back then, but we had essentially been conditioned or, you could say, brainwashed, into believing there was only one way to educate our children. Therefore, a process of 'de-programming' was needed!*

*Could it really be the case that simply doing 'nothing' or* 'not a lot' was the next step? How hard could this be? Well, in practise not hard at all. There were no more early mornings. There were no absolutely rigid bedtimes. We had single-handedly removed the panicking about what hadn't been done the night before. There were no PE kits, no packed lunches, no hands up in class, no worrying about not knowing the answer. There was no school run. The only school run was to the kitchen or the lounge. There was no homework. By-and-large there was no 'work' at all. The point of de-schooling is to replace 'work' with a sense of play and – if done cleverly – the point of all the play is to indirectly 'learn' without any effort.

Here was a chance to get know my child again. And when I think back to these first days, they were some of most meaningful and rewarding I think I've ever had as a parent. We would snuggle up and read together whenever we wanted to. There was no nagging. No cajoling. We didn't have those frantic early morning rush-throughs of homework that Kiki had forgotten to tell us about. We could kick back and watch kid-friendly documentaries, which was great because I finally got to watch all of the Blue Planet films with her. The joy of homeschooling is that you get to spend precious time with your children that was previously allocated to teachers.

I think this is probably something many parents have discovered through lockdown and though they may not want to homeschool full time, I think many feel a little sad about a return to 'normal' and all that it entails: crazy schedules, not enough time, countless deadlines, etc. We constantly hear stories in the press about how stressed and anxious young children are, and I would wager all the money in the world that the lion's share of this stress is directly attributable to the academic and social demands of school.

When Kiki landed in my lap in those early days, she was sleep-deprived. She had missed so much sleep due to her worries around school. Being patched. Being the youngest in her year. Being shy. She was still having night terrors, but they were definitely lessening. And she started to get her appetite back, albeit slowly.

Me and Mark meanwhile were having more sleepless nights for very different reasons. Although I could feel Kiki was definitely starting to trust me again and that the bond between us was deepening, I was also totally overwhelmed with an enormous dose of parent's guilt about what she had been through. Mark, meanwhile, was having night terrors for an entirely different reason.

## Mark

As I've said, although I knew we had no choice but to take this drastic action, I was absolutely petrified. I would lie awake at night, sometimes on my own, because Kiki was still so unsettled in the early days that when she got her night terrors she would climb into bed with Nadia. I would pad across the house to sleep with the dogs, and just lie there looking at the ceiling! Having battled my own addiction to alcohol, I was feeling all the symptoms of detox. Good old-fashioned detox. I felt breathless, shaky, restless, disturbed and agitated. Night after night, as Nadia repeated her mantra of 'Relax, Mark we are de-schooling' (I have to admit she was particularly annoying), I slowly began to realise that the only real problem at this moment in time was me!

There was nothing for it. I had to admit powerlessness. I couldn't keep swimming in Lake Denial. I was addicted to the rules, the timetable, the academic targets, the syllabuses . . . the entire concept of the school system. However much I could understand the need to pull Kiki out of school, I was basically hooked on the system, and I felt totally at sea.

Here's a snapshot of what was going on in my head: fine, we're having to circumnavigate things for a bit, perhaps even go 'off-road' for a short while, but in the back of my mind I was adamant that we would be returning back to GCSE business-as-usual at a later stage in our girls' lives. As far as I was concerned, Nadia was doing this thing called de-schooling back at home (she had more flexibility and time at this stage than me), and if I'm honest, although I said I understood and agreed, I was far from satisfied. No doubt, like many parents who recently went into lockdown, I was in a private state of panic. I was looking for all the textbooks and worksheets that best approximated what Kiki would have been learning at this stage at school. Amazon parcels were arriving that weighed a ton and were laden with Key Stage 2 books on every conceivable subject. In my head the mantra ran, 'We HAVE to keep the INFORMATION going

IN!! We HAVE to keep the INFORMATION going IN!!'
When Nadia saw these piles of books arriving, she would
calmly remind me, 'Mark, not yet. Put those boxes in your
office - we're de-schooling. YOU need to de-school too.'

I felt like I was in purgatory . . . but as things continued
. . . so too was I gradually de-schooled.

## Nadia

I really felt for Mark in these early days. I could see he was
being pulled in opposite directions. Wanting the best for Kiki
emotionally and psychologically, but not able to see a way
that didn't include eventually returning to the conventional
milestones of GCSEs and A Levels. That's not to say I didn't
want Kiki to follow this path too, but we were in a critical
situation and my instinct was telling me that in the short
term all bets were off. We were firefighting again, and I felt
confident that there would be time to work out what we
would actually do in the long term at a later stage. Right
now. Right here. This was the only right decision. We
ensured we went to even more galleries and museums than
usual. We would sit with Kiki and spend time online searching
for whatever things gave her a spark of joy. Lots and lots of
time and patience getting her to open up about how she felt.
It was agonisingly slow.

•

It's important to stress that de-schooling isn't about simply sitting back and doing absolutely nothing. The prospect of lounging around on sofas and being bored at home was probably what was worrying both of us at the beginning. We discovered that de-schooling is all about removing the set-dressing of school. The rules. The time limits. The times tables. The speed with which things are done or learnt. It's essentially about opening up our children and us as parents to the idea that learning doesn't have to occur simply within a classroom setting. So many elements of the classroom setting are anathema to free and easy learning. There's noise and distraction. The teacher is spread among many students. And there is the constant drumbeat of impending SATs and the demands of Ofsted and the curriculum.

A dear friend of ours, who used to be a teacher in a school not dissimilar to the one Maddie and Kiki encountered, once told us that he calculated the amount of dedicated one-on-one time he felt each of his students got with him during an ordinary class. It was something like forty-seven seconds!

Classrooms necessarily make learning an uneven experience for children. If you're the kind of kid who doesn't like putting your hand up to answer questions there is a sense that you are *not* learning. The school setting can be a traumatic place for some kids – especially shy or quieter kids.

We hold no store with the concept that school is all

about knocking the sides off your children and toughening them up for life. Yes, children need to know how things will be in the world, but they are also entitled to be taken through the experience of finding this stuff out in a way that better suits their individual personalities and educational needs. Through no fault of its own, the educational system, and the systems at work in individual schools, *have* to find some kind of happy medium that will work for *most* of the kids. Most classrooms settle on a level of teaching that suits the majority in a class. This necessarily leaves the *brightest* and the *struggling* somewhat unattended.

Where this approach encounters difficulties is when we (as parents) can see the harm it's doing, and decide we don't want our kids to be treated in this one-size-fits-all way. It's fine if it works (as with our eldest girls Issy and Fleur), but if it doesn't, there needs to be an alternative option. Homeschooling in all its many guises *can* offer that option.

Key to understanding de-schooling is *not* thinking of it as a period of *no learning*. To de-school is not to say that you will *stop* learning. Quite the opposite. In fact, de-schooling at its best can manifest in microcosm some of the most liberating tenets of homeschooling in general. De-schooling is about removing the rules and regulations placed around learning in a school environment. De-schooling is about getting your child and *you* to lose those old habitual ways of thinking about learning. It doesn't have to start at nine a.m. It doesn't have to stop at three p.m. It doesn't have to happen in forty-minute sessions. Playtime doesn't have to be just ten minutes. De-schooling is an opportunity to do what we believe is the most critically important first thing you *need* to do when reconsidering the ways in which your children are going to be educated: getting to *know* your child. It may sound simple, but we never cease to be amazed by how perplexed so many parents are when we say to them 'get to know your child'. Even the most liberal-minded of parents like to think they know *precisely* who their kids are, when quite often they probably don't.

Nearly every family falls foul of pigeonholing family members. We have done it over the years – and one of the first things de-schooling teaches you as a parent (before its even taught your child a single thing) is that *defining* a child is one of the most reductive things you can do.

You'll often hear phrases like, 'Oh Johnny – he's the academic one' . . . 'Sarah – she's the sporty one' . . . 'Simon is only really any good with his hands' . . . 'She's the bookworm' . . . 'He's not very academic' . . . *All* these phrases, all these definitions; in using them, what we are doing without even realising it is trying to lock our children in to some sort of preordained destiny. Maybe Simon isn't a reader of books because he's been given the wrong books at the wrong time? Maybe Sarah's sporty because academic subjects have been delivered to her in a way that bears no relationship to everyday life? Maybe he isn't a maths genius because he hasn't yet been shown the mathematical beauty at the heart of architecture or illustration?

None of these type-castings are born of malice. We often wonder whether the desire to control our children's destiny perhaps comes from the primal fear we have as parents that this thing called 'grown-up life' is in itself such an ever-shifting, contradictory, highly unreliable and changeable concept. So as best as we can, we try to pin down, to lock in what we *know* about our kids at an early age in order to try and better equip them to deal with whatever the world may throw at them. Because we cannot ever do this completely, there's a sort of security in pre-defining your kids as academic or practical or physical from as early an age as possible. In some strange way, we believe this might secure their destinies and protect them from the world.

## You're only young once

De-schooling is *all* about exploding these ways of viewing our children and their learning. It's akin to throwing everything in the air and waiting for it all to settle on the ground around us. As soon as you have your child in front of you and you're de-schooling, let them *daydream*! Let them step towards *all* their passions or interests. What on earth happened to the phrase that used to be bandied about by adults back in the seventies . . . 'You're only young once'? All too often in today's world, children are being asked to sacrifice their childhoods based on their parents' fears of adulthood.

We all think we know our children, and no doubt the absolute panic-stations that many families have experienced during the recent coronavirus pandemic was as much about the fear of spending too much time with our children as it was about how on earth we are going to teach them. It's important to acknowledge that homeschooling (in any of its myriad different forms) is *not* for everyone. Some parents do *not* want to *know* their children any more than they currently do and that modern-day living allows.

Many people we know have said to us, 'OH MY GOD! I couldn't think of anything worse than spending all day with my kids!' Which always comes as a shock to us; we *love* spending time with our girls (obviously not *all* the time). But then one of the biggest myths about homeschooling is the idea that you will be spending *all* your time with your children. You won't, and you don't. It's not good for them or you. But knowing your children more, or better – how can that ever be a bad thing?

For many parents, the concept of getting to 'know' your kids will conjure up images of happy-clappy sandal-wearing hippies all holding hands and singing 'Kumbaya, My Lord'. And for many parents, a lot of what we are about to discuss will be akin to talking double Dutch – and that's *okay*. But we would urge anyone with an interest in learning and education to just pause and consider whether the system as it currently operates sufficiently provides for *your* children.

If, like us, you have the capacity to enact change, or want to simply reconsider what exactly it is that you want education to be for your children, de-schooling has a lot going for it.

To get a readily manageable grab on de-schooling and what it is or can be, take a look at the summer holidays that most kids and their families have every year, plonked at the end of the academic year. Is it not the time we are all dashing for and secretly working towards? In many ways you could argue that the summer months are a little like a state-sanctioned period of time in the year when kids, and sometimes parents, can de-compress – and de-school. Very often in the summer holidays, kids go through the normal gamut of feeling bored, then being inventive, being non-communicative with us parents, and then having moments of great intimacy. Sometimes new friendships can be formed, and new experiences can be had.

At its simplest de-schooling is all of this and more, just for a slightly longer period of time. Not only does the child benefit from de-schooling . . . the parent does too.

## Mark

*My fear during those early days (like that of many parents in lockdown) was that just a week or two without any formal education could result in Kiki slipping 'too far behind'. Given that Nadia was talking in terms of months . . . the fear of falling behind was constantly bouncing around my stressed mind.*

*As time ticked past, and we moved into a few weeks and the first month, I suppose I must have started to experience the effects of de-schooling on the parent mind. Very slowly I began to question this concept of 'falling behind'. Behind what? What arbitrary measures and yardsticks were we using to gauge the so-called 'success' of our daughter? I'd start the thought cocksure and confident - before quickly slipping back into worry and finding myself on the government website outlining the recommended English syllabus for year 5 and year 6 children (all 136 pages of it) . . . I'd end up printing them off and storing them in my desk for later reference. Once Nadia had got past this insane de-schooling period - I would have the firepower to start cramming knowledge into Kiki's head again.*

As you can tell, I was slow in coming to homeschooling. Which is why it's all the more remarkable that as I sit here now looking back, I have not a shred of doubt about the all the subsequent choices we made in Maddie and Kiki's home-schooling journey.

Like an engine spurting into action, I started to develop ideas that could possibly encourage gentle learning without upsetting the de-schooling apple cart.

One thing I DID know as an English graduate was that reading Tom's Midnight Garden was in no way going to fire up Kiki's imagination. So, during this period of de-schooling we did (believe it or not) allow Kiki to watch lots of cartoons - Adventure Time, The Regular Show, The Amazing World of Gumball. I remembered as a boy really enjoying reading the novels that were written off the back of films. I think the first book I read was a paperback version of the Disney film Bambi. Using visual references as a pre-cursor to reading a book - or harnessing a kid's imagination with a visual world that's already been created - allows them to indirectly understand how the written word can describe or bring to life the visuals. So, I took Kiki along to my favourite comic shop in Covent Garden and said, 'We aren't going to read a single book - we are going to buy the comic books of all the cartoon shows you've been watching at home.' I remember her looking wide-eyed at the thought that this could be considered 'reading'. To this day, graphic novels and comics are a mainstay of most young adults' material. Comics have the additional attributes of showing how to storyboard and structure a story. Our use of comic books was just one way of trying to invisibly substitute a very stressful sort of learning around literacy with something more fun, less rules-based, and with a multimedia feel to it. To this day Kiki is still drawn to creating works of art inspired by comics and graphic novels, and of course these days there's something known as 'Geek Chic'. Embrace it!

## Nadia

Even though we were de-schooling without any formal learning, there were, of course, lots of opportunities to facilitate Kiki's learning without her realising. As cooking is something that I love to do, I set about getting Kiki into the kitchen with me. This was not only a really fun way for us to spend time together and for me to share my limited skills with her, but it was also a chance for her to learn unlimited skills. Cooking is a very organic way to incorporate all kinds of subjects, from maths to biology to geography – and what I didn't realise is that the list is endless.

There's a fair amount of problem-solving involved when following a recipe and cooking. It involves lots of maths! I would sometimes pretend that we would only need half the recipe so that we could work out how to do that. We would also work out how to turn temperatures from Fahrenheit to centigrade. All of this involves division, fractions, adding, subtracting. We would discuss the cost of everything and try to work out how much a dish was costing us to make.

Cooking is also about chemistry, science, and biology. You have to make predictions and try and understand the changes that happen to ingredients (chemicals) when you cook them. We are sowing the seeds for an interest in chemistry - for, after all, most of cooking is chemistry: heating, freezing, mixing and blending are all processes used both in a laboratory and a kitchen. When we cook food, a whole host of different physical and chemical processes happen. It was exciting to watch Kiki's fascination with the magic that goes on in the kitchen - whisking egg whites and sugar to make meringue; watching liquids turn to solids, such as turning a raw egg into a solid omelette; making a custard with egg and cream and then freezing it into ice cream; activating yeast with warm liquid and sugar, then mixing it with flour to watch it grow and then making bread with it.

We also covered human biology subjects in a very casual way, by talking about different food groups and how they work in our body. For example, we might make a potato dish and I would talk about carbohydrates and their effect on the body, and the same again for proteins and fats. We would talk about what was good for us and learn about vitamins and minerals, and of course about what is not so good for us. What is the importance of each of the five senses? Do we eat with our eyes - yes, that's very important, but is it more important than taste and smell? Is touch important at all? Is it important to hear the sound of an apple, a carrot or a stick of celery crunching when we bite into it?

I would also surreptitiously incorporate geography, by talking about where different foods grow and the climates that different foods need to thrive. We would talk, too, about the diets of people in different countries and how they make use of their particular foods, such as Mexico and its corn, Asia and its many varieties of spices, Egypt and its beans and pulses; even the regional differences within a country: the South of France with its olive oil, the north with its butter, the dozens of differences across the wide sweep of the USA, India, China . . . We would research and cook foods from different countries and try to learn some of the ingredients in the words of each country. This would often end in hilarity, although at this stage it was upsetting to see that Kiki was still hesitant and jittery around answering anything in case she got it wrong.

We would talk a bit, so as to not overwhelm her, about the history of different recipes, and food history through the ages. Kiki was already on her way to becoming a confident cook but was still very nervous in case she made a mistake. Although at first I found this frustrating, I realised quite quickly that no amount of impatience could ever work with Kiki. Impatience is what makes a lot of children who need more time on things at school get more and more stressed. I found a neat visual way for her to process these recipes and processes, which involved her writing everything down and drawing her own pictures to accompany her recipes.

*This simple process encouraged handwriting, vocabulary and design skills.*

•

We weren't formally teaching in either of these scenarios, we were simply placing Kiki alongside experiences and allowing 'stuff' to rub off on her – allowing knowledge to seep in. Now, whether all this knowledge would stay with her was another matter. But as a strategy, it's only now when we look back that we can sort of pat ourselves on the back and consider that we had perhaps made some sensible decisions during her de-schooling. Throughout this period Mark continued to take the girls to galleries and theatres and the cinema, but it was never presented as a lesson or even a homeschooling trip. It just became part of our lives. While Nadia was focussing on cookery for stealth learning and Mark was using comics and graphic novels to try to radically change the concept of reading for Kiki, we both were aware that art offers up probably the widest variety of ways to transform how children see and interpret the world around them. Art in its infinite different guises has a remarkable capacity to feed a child's imagination.

We are *not* talking about going to the National Gallery and studying the greats in a dry and fusty way that leads to 'museum legs'. No. If you're blessed with an urban centre somewhere near you, anywhere near you, hunt out the young artists, the public artists, the graffiti artists, the performance artists. We live on the outskirts of London, and every single day of the week there is some weird or whacked-out exhibition or show by some strange artist. When Kiki was very young, we would take her to (free) site-specific exhibitions where a council flat had been transformed into a cave of sparkly blue crystal courtesy of some magical chemical reaction. We'd take them to Tate Modern and they would hurtle down the enormous slide from the top of the Turbine Hall to the ground. We'd find a Damien Hirst show and get them to stand face to face with a pickled shark. Kids like to be shocked. Kids like to be scared. Kids will suddenly want to go out if they know there's the possibility of something unexpected. This was how Mark approached the arts with all his daughters. Being *open-minded* as a parent is critical – because at the end of the day by electing to homeschool in any way you are wanting to quite literally *open* your child's *minds* to the full potential of the world.

There is *nothing* more rewarding than the moment a child realises there *aren't* any strict rules when it comes to what they could see in an art gallery. The idea that rules can be broken is *radical* in the creative minds of children. It's also really fun to bamboozle them even more by telling them that one of our most notorious artists (Damien Hirst) failed his art exams. If you can keep an open mind to *all* the arts, this will help immeasurably when it comes to your child's inclination to learn and find out more. Remember, even art and creativity can engage with the sciences, and often engineering too. And so, by stealth, more than *one* subject can be engaged with through art alone.

But if there is one thing we have struggled with over the years, it's how to banish from our children's minds and hearts the idea that getting things wrong is bad. Only by repeatedly failing can you find success. Sometimes the greatest success resides in failure. These ideas or maxims might resonate for us adults – but try telling a child that a really average, or even frustratingly bad drawing of a still life is a crucial stepping stone to getting it right, when they've just come from a school in which there will always be someone or a few people who are constantly excelling beyond the rest. This was one of the most difficult hangovers to cure for our girls, and to this day it is still a work in progress. It's really hard to keep a child's interest in a subject or an activity if they keep struggling at it. But one thing is for sure, you stand more chance of getting them round or over these hurdles if they're not having to *keep up* with the rest of the class. We must all remember that phrase in parents' evenings – 'he or she is struggling to keep up with the rest of the class'. The inference being that if you can't keep up you're slow, and you risk being left behind.

# Finding our feet
# with our youngest

---

*Curiosity is the engine of achievement.*

*Sir Ken Robinson*

---

Just as Kiki's homeschooling journey was coming out of the de-schooling zone, we both knew we were doing the right thing for her. Interestingly, we weren't quite connecting the dots and thinking that perhaps the same solution could work for Maddie. Not yet.

**Nadia**

*Something called SLHE (The South London Home Education) email group became a lifeline for me. Most regions of the*

UK have their own online homeschooling group. It works very much like a noticeboard. It was (and still is) a really reliable and informative place where no matter what question I asked, a flood of answers would always come back. Now, you have to be invited to these groups. Home-ed parents are fiercely protective of the rights they feel they've fought for, and its important you go into these forums respecting this fact.

Every morning, an email will land in my inbox with a full list of activities, support groups, day trips, visits – you name it. Given that socialising is one of the biggest concerns most parents have about homeschooling their children, it was a hugely welcome relief to find out quite quickly that there were dozens and dozens of groups, classes and get-togethers for homeschooled kids.

This is where I found the first group for Kiki. It was held in a bizarre building for young cadets. It involved a very long train journey and two buses followed by a whole day spent in the classroom. The difference to school was that, because Kiki wouldn't let me leave her (not even for a minute), the teachers would sympathetically let me stay for as long as she wanted. Me and Kiki went here for several terms, but not once did she let me leave her. It began to slowly dawn on me that her experiences at school and the trauma she felt as a consequence were not going to simply fade away. She had developed a phobia of teachers and being taught on her own in a class environment. This was when I started to consider that we were maybe going to need some extra help from a professional.

*In these weekly classes, she did art, science and nature, Greek mythology and drama (which meant I did too!). I absolutely loved the teaching there. I loved the fact that the teachers weren't intimidated by me being in the class, that they were open to the fact that me and Kiki essentially needed special measures. The kids were all incredibly confident and frighteningly smart – and I mean frighteningly smart. This is a really important point to make: one of the things I've noticed over the years is that homeschooled kids have a certain spark or light behind their eyes. They can be frighteningly driven – which in its own way can be a problem of sorts for an introvert like Kiki. But – and this is where not being in a school setting is an advantage – Kiki wasn't having to 'keep up' with them. She wasn't 'falling behind', because everyone was essentially going at their own pace.*

*These lessons were very noisy and bombastic, but the teachers never shouted and the kids adored them. In fact, the teachers seemed to relish this noisy enthusiasm and there was a genuine sense of controlled chaos. The teachers went to great lengths in creating an atmosphere of inclusivity. There was no shaming. No streaming. No shouting. And no real sense of right or wrong. We were all just learning together! It was heaven.*

*With Mark fretting about the potential lack of structure and order to homeschooling, I leant on him to attend these classes just once to see for himself.*

## Mark

*In these early days I remember going to a couple of the 'hang outs' Nadia was taking Kiki to. One was an adventure playground where a group of homeschooling mums would bring their kids to run riot. Kiki developed some of her earliest friendships in homeschooling here. I do remember feeling very intimidated when I went along to see what it was all about, but when I got there, I discovered just ordinary mums all talking about this or that group their kids were going to, this or that course or extra-curricular activity they were pursuing. It wasn't an atmosphere of happy-clappy sandal-wearing hippies all wanting to sit in a circle and plait each others' hair. These were real parents like me and Nadia from all walks of life, with their own compelling stories about why they'd elected to homeschool their kids. The other place I remember heading off to was the Kingston class Nadia describes. Now, it's important to remember that when I headed along to this day class or that day school – I was carrying all of my fears surrounding the idea that unless Kiki was taught in a structured and school-like fashion she wasn't going to learn anything. I had all the prejudices and fears of someone who had too much skin in the game when it came to conventional learning.*

*I remember when I walked through the door I was greeted with a wall of sound so loud I didn't know what had hit me. I was reeling. Across the day, as the wonderful supervisors (themselves ex-teachers and ex-teaching assistants)* moved the kids from subject to subject, through physical games as much as mental challenges, I remember being slowly drawn into the magic of what was going on. I could see that because Kiki was nervous about fully joining in, she needed me to become more involved in things; a really important thing to recognise. If you are struggling (like we were) with a child who doesn't feel they can get involved fully - try and be willing to make a tit of yourself. That is precisely what I did. By the end of the day, I remember hosting and helping with a project all about fashion through the ages and what different people were wearing at different times in their lives. The less I worried about getting involved, the more Kiki laughed and slowly came out of her shell. Nadia was a natural at jumping up and getting stuck in, but sometimes it's really important for us as parents to recognise that we too, as adults, can be nervy and hesitant and that our kids are often looking to us for inspiration in these social situations.

One other class that I solely used to take Kiki to was something called 'Maths Explorers', which was a locally run maths group that would take place in local cafes. A group of kids would all gather and a lovely team of ex-teachers (and active teachers) would find inclusive and essentially less boring ways to teach youngsters maths. This was something that Kiki came to nervously, but, once again, because I was allowed to be in the class (which wouldn't be allowed at school) and because the classes were often on Saturday mornings - it was easy for us to learn together.

## Nadia

*After a while, however, I realised that the travel was getting me down, and so I was inspired to open our own home-schooling group within an annexe in my parent's house next door to us. It was empty, spacious, close to home (ha ha) and allowed me and Mark to continue working from home. (At that time Mark often had a six-person production team tromping around our house!!)*

*Northwood Heights was born. We decided to use the Kingston model as inspiration, and create a unique learning environment for young people that would help them explore and lead with their own inquisitiveness at a pace that suited them best. Our ethos was to offer these children (and by extension their parents) an unhurried, creative and motivational learning environment where everyone can find real joy in learning and experience the richness of life. Ambitious, heh?*

*Each day would use the creative arts as a way to bring to the surface the individual creativity of each child. It was our belief that a creative education could cover such areas of artistic expression as drama, movement, philosophy and debating, while professionally and discreetly incorporating all the known core subjects.*

*Every half term a painting and an artist would be the focus for the breadth of the entire learning experience. We would explore the painting through the lenses of history, geography, influences, critics, etc. In allowing children the time to question and think about the artwork in question, the sessions prioritised conveying information while allowing time for reflection, as well as the opportunity to process things in a calm and relaxing environment. The aim was to find interdisciplinary approaches to the art and the artist – including forays into such areas as geometry, mathematics, science, geography, the science and philosophy of colour, and religion along the way.*

*By adopting an open-ended academic approach to something as simple as an artwork or an artist, we would allow learning to mushroom outwards towards all other subjects. In this way, children would find themselves chewing over subject areas they perhaps wouldn't ordinarily find themselves comfortable exploring. Helping us in this endeavour was a small team of three former teachers who were themselves looking for an alternative environment in which to utilise their teaching skills more calmly and gently.*

*Over time, small groups came to be run with tutors, Arts Awards were organised by a brilliantly avant-garde young artist and teaching assistant. The debating class covered anything and everything and would often take something in the news as a starting point for discussion.*

*Although the debates proper happened at Northwood Heights, we would of course spend time discussing the topics over dinner as a family. Many families avoid discussing the news with their children, but we actively do the opposite. We use the news as a chance to try and educate. Brexit was brilliant for discussing the structure and make up of Europe and the history of post-war Europe.*

## Mark

*Throughout this time Kiki was still dealing with extreme anxiety, and Nadia had to stay alongside her in virtually every lesson. Naturally this was a bind, but key to these early days was adopting a more patient attitude to learning.*

*There were many other strange and wonderful places that Nadia took the girls to – one of them being forest school, where the girls got to hug trees, make fires and whittle wood. They told me over dinner that they didn't really take to it, in fact they hated it – but it sounded brilliant to me! I would have loved it! But this is one of the most wonderful elements of homeschooling: maintaining a sense of humour around the failed attempts to engage the children as well as the successes.*

*Far from having limited options as a homeschooler, on a daily basis our online updates from SLHE forum deliver us an Aladdin's cave of options. Across the length and breadth of the country, countless homeschooling groups in countless disciplines, for different levels and age groups, are being run by dedicated and passionate parents and teachers. There are even incredibly niche courses for incredibly niche interests – everything from comic-book design to stop-frame animation to physics and chemistry at the Khan Institute, going on day trips to the "centre of the cell" in Central London. Courses approach subjects in the unlikeliest of ways – whether it be through the lenses of textiles, Minecraft, music, dance or drama. Parents publicise homeschooling trips to museums* or galleries that offer special guides and worksheets for home-schooling groups. Of course, the great thing about these trips is that they are often outside the hours that mainstream schools visit these attractions – so as a group you'll invariably have the venue to yourselves. There are countless classes for sporty kids: gymnastics, dance, football, tennis, squash, table tennis and, of course, that homeschooling staple – skate-boarding!! There are also the more unusual outings that schools are just not set up to do – trips to places such as Kew Gardens, zoos, animal rescue centres, or even taking first-aid CPR courses. Certain venues find they cannot accom-modate the enormous class sizes that come from most schools, but the prospect of smaller homeschool groups of between four and six kids is infinitely more manageable. We even came across one notice that invited homeschooled teenagers to hook up (under the supervision of a homeschooling parent) and explore a new route around a certain part of London that featured public artworks and graffiti all by themselves.

# Bullying as a cause
# for change

## Pulling Maddie out of school
## and getting to know our eldest

Some parents turn to homeschooling as a last resort and not as an ideological choice. Sadly, bullying is a common reason why parents take their children out of school. When we decided that Maddie needed to come out of school, we were fortunate in that we already had Kiki at home. We sort of knew what to expect on a macro level. But, once again, we found ourselves dealing with a child who had – for different reasons – been traumatised by the system.

## Nadia

*Moving Maddie from primary school to stage school felt like an absolute whirlwind. It had been so shocking and upsetting to hear how unhappy she'd been without us knowing that we felt we had no option but to move her. And quite quickly, a sense of doom gave way to possibility. It was such an exciting moment when she was offered a place in stage school, that, with hindsight, I wonder if we let our relief cloud our judgement. Within a matter of weeks, we had gone from feeling quite desperate about her future to being offered this great chance. After our meeting with her primary-school headmaster, who had given us a bleak outlook about her academic future, we were suddenly being told by her new principal that because (according to the stage school's assessment) she was ahead academically, it was advisable she go into a year above her age group. I think we were so happy and relieved to hear something positive about her academically, that we didn't really take on board the possible social implications that she might face by spending so much time with children a whole year older than her.*

*Maddie says that her first six months or so at the school were relatively happy. She was top of the class academically, and she was doing really well in all her vocational classes. I think Mark and I probably felt very proud of ourselves at this point. We believed a hundred per cent that we'd done the right thing in moving her. But, as we were to discover,* we had only been firefighting, and things were about to get very difficult indeed.

But let's just sit with the good times for a moment. We absolutely loved the energy of this new, very small school, where it seemed every single child wanted to be there more than anything else in the world. It was so different from Maddie's previous school, where everything had been very formal and staid. There were only about a hundred pupils in the whole school, so no more than ten in a class. We were thrilled about this, and on top of it, we found the atmosphere and cacophony of sound that hit us whenever we went there completely intoxicating. This was the right school, thank God! We really felt that only great things could happen here.

## Mark

Nadia is right. We knew that the only things that really made Maddie's heart sing (quite literally) involved perform-ance. She was brilliant at Stagecoach (which she'd attended since the age of six), she loved her music, she loved to dance (two nights a week she'd choreograph and dance for the family of her own free will) and she absolutely adored her films.

What on earth wasn't there to like about stage school? With our early-day experiences of Kiki coursing through our veins, and the words of Ken Robinson ricocheting around her heads, I viewed the mistake of prep school and the move to stage school as a manifestation of us getting something right after having first got it wrong!

*Being told she was academically ahead of things in a different school showed me how off the scale her prep school's academic expectations had been. It also reminded me that the perception of 'intellect' and 'intelligence' was subjective from institution to institution.*

*I felt we had landed on our feet. We were still coming to terms with Kiki at home de-schooling and so the thought that Maddie might have found her calling was a Godsend. I vividly remember dropping Maddie off at school most mornings and hearing the sounds of her singing classes and dance classes from the street, a huge part of me smiling to think that Maddie was now doing precisely what she wanted to do. In a weird way, again with the benefit of hindsight, this move from a highly academic prep school over to a performing-arts stage school was the first inadvertent step taken towards homeschooling Maddie too. You could say we got there in stages, and this was the first stage. In other words, recognising that the child in question was defined by a love of performing.*

## Nadia

*But this school was by no means a soft option. School started at eight a.m. and finished at five p.m. The mornings were spent on all the academic subjects, preparing for eight GCSEs. In the afternoons the children worked hard on jazz, ballet, tap, singing, drama and voice production. We were thrilled that she was working so hard and seemed really focused. It* also seemed that she had made lots of friends and everything was tickety-boo.

Were our egos at play here? Were we just seeing what we wanted to see? As we were to discover, most of the children were highly competitive, ambitious, and, dare I say it, precocious. I don't think we realised that Maddie was starting to struggle with spending such long days with children who were not only older than her, but also much more worldly wise.

Maddie and I were talking about this recently and she said that when she first arrived there, it was a shock, because she'd been in such a closeted world in primary school, where everybody spoke to each other so nicely. No swearing, nobody had a mobile phone or wore make-up or talked about having a boyfriend. At stage school she had really felt like a fish out of water, that she was really behind socially. She had never had a phone, didn't have a clue about Instagram or anything else the other kids were always talking about.

This was just the beginning of the problems that she was going to face when it came to bullying. In fact, Maddie says, with hindsight, the bullying began in a subtle way, within a week of her being there, but because everything was so new and scary, she didn't realise what was going on. It breaks my heart that when we really drilled into what was behind the bullying, although we found out it stemmed from a number of things, the principal cause was that I was 'off the telly'.

Maddie says that the fact that the classes were so small

made it easy for the two bullies to control the whole class. Maddie tells me that the minute she arrived at school she would know if it was going to be a day when she was spoken to or given the silent treatment by the whole class. The 'popular' girls were very manipulative, and, as Maddie herself admits, she was too immature to know how to deal with it. Initially she pretended to us that everything was fine. Then, one night, I went in to give her a kiss goodnight, and just asked her how her day had gone, and to my absolute horror, she told me how she was being treated and that she was really unhappy. My heart sank because although she didn't know how to articulate it, she was being bullied. I knew from what she'd told me that she was. I also knew, as every parent does, that bullying is one of the most difficult things to deal with. I felt so sad for her and for us. We hadn't solved a problem, we had simply swapped it for another one. I felt so sad that she had kept all this to herself because, as she said, 'I didn't want to tell you and Daddy, because everyone's so happy that I'm going to this school.'

The next day I booked an appointment with the headmistress. In contrast to our meetings with the other headmaster, I felt it was very good and that she had really listened and, more importantly, heard us, and she promised us she would look into it.

I left the school feeling pretty proud of myself (idiot!) that I had dealt with this very quickly. I felt hopeful for the future. What an IDIOT!

*Six weeks or so later, I entered the celebrity* Big Brother *house, expecting to have a bit of a jolly jape and hopefully be evicted within the first week so I could get back to my family. How wrong could I have been?! That year's series was one of the most dramatic in the series' history. While in the* Big Brother *house I witnessed some of the worst bullying I've ever seen in my life. Each episode was more explosive than the one before. The goings-on were on the front of every newspaper, and everyone was talking about it. It was hell on earth inside, but I had no idea of the impact it was having on the outside, or the ramifications it was having for Maddie.*

## Mark

*Little did we know what a challenge Nadia doing* Big Brother *was going present to us as a family. Firstly, going on a reality show isn't the kind of thing most families routinely experience. So, there was no guidebook on how to manage the experience as we sat on the outside of the* Big Brother *house looking in. On a practical level, we had a number of classes, tutors and child carers on hand to help with Kiki at home while I was working (more about the detail of this later), and in principle Maddie was going to be fine heading off to school most mornings. Except it slowly dawned on me that she was anything but fine.*

*We'd had the drama of me and Nadia going in to meet the headmistress about bullying, but it started to become apparent that things weren't running smoothly. Sadly, as is the way with bullies, the girls at the school who had already managed to manipulate and play with Maddie's emotions could smell blood! They knew her mother was unavailable and essentially trapped in television, and as the series became more and more dramatic it was the only thing the tabloid newspapers and by extension all the kids at Maddie's school were talking about. As the bullying on our TV screens reached dramatic proportions, it would seem that something similar was getting worse at Maddie's school.*

*Rather than trying to go the headmistress route again, imploring the school to do something about it, I elected for direct action. I reached out to the bully's mother and requested a stop to the behaviour . . . Of course - as is the way with systemic bullying in a school - any attempt at resolving the problem only resulted in a more twisted and insidious form of bullying. Whether it be the silent treatment, or the whispers, or the huddled groups, our idyllic solution to Maddie's schooling was beginning to take a very dark and twisted turn, much like Nadia's experience on our TV sets each evening.*

*It was horrific. Lacking the finesse and emotional sophistication of a mother, my way was to try and solve things directly by simply telling the parents in question what was happening and requesting it to STOP! Naturally, bullying isn't resolved like this. It never is. It didn't stop - it just got driven underground and became more underhand.*

●

When Nadia returned to the real world, we both began to realise that it would be very difficult for the school Maddie was at to deal effectively with the bullying. For anyone who has experienced bullying in a school setting, the sense of helplessness is profoundly debilitating. We implored, we pleaded, we reached out – but once they've started, nothing can stop children of a certain age (riven with whatever their own issues are) from bullying (however low level) another child. The drip, drip effect on Maddie was heart-breaking, and the reality of the situation dawned on us. What felt like a lifeline for our eldest was now an albatross around her neck and ours.

When a bullying problem gets entrenched at a school, it doesn't matter what you do; it will never change. We have spoken to many teachers about this over the years and they pretty much all have confirmed that they have rarely ever seen a successful resolution.

In fact, we would probably go so far as to say that if *your* child is being systematically bullied, and there appears to be no way of resolving it at least in the short term, just move your child out of the toxic situation, and then we'd suggest you consider homeschooling. Take the plunge. You won't regret it.

That said, managing your child's education is *never* the easiest choice. It is going to require a *lot* of legwork, a *lot* of time and a *lot* of care and attention. But as a short-term solution to a bullying crisis, it is an entirely legal and appropriate move to make.

## When the going gets tough . . .

We can all make the judgement as parents when it comes to the resilience of our children. We would never say to simply turn your back on a challenging situation the first time you encounter it. Whether your child goes to school or ends up being homeschooled in some way, the need for resilience, perseverance and bravery is a natural part of life. Quite understandably, many parents may fear that making their children's problems disappear rather than encouraging them to solve them for themselves means they won't 'toughen up' for life. But is survival of the fittest necessarily the best route for *all* children? We don't think so. We also believe that *most* parents know when they've gone down every avenue and tried every solution. When you feel there's nowhere left to turn and that the school is powerless to resolve a bullying problem, remember homeschooling is an entirely legal and quite immediate solution.

# To GCSE or not to GCSE?

When Maddie eventually came out of school, she had already been witnessing the relative freedom that Kiki was encountering as a homeschooled child. The challenges we faced with Maddie came with the fact that she was much older and her academic path was more naturally heading towards, if not knocking on the doors of, GCSEs . . . that Holy Grail of qualifications, a very clear and shining beacon that signals how well – or badly – educated you are. As Maddie recently told us, 'My friends believe that if you don't get good grades in your GCSEs your life is effectively over.'

The thorny subject of GCSEs is a tricky one, and it is often the stick with which those who doubt homeschooling hit us the hardest. It seems there's no easy discussion about these qualifications. Our relationship with GCSEs and Maddie has been one shrouded in stress, self-doubt, confusion and (if we so say ourselves) littered with a lack of coherence which hasn't always been great . . . BUT at the beginning of Maddie's homeschooling we kept things simple (just like we did with Kiki before her).

## Nadia

*When we decided to pull Maddie out of school we didn't experience the same pink cloud of euphoria that we did with Kiki. Instead we felt defeated. Maddie had used to play an awful lot with Kiki before she went to stage school, and Kiki thought she'd be getting her playful sister back. But Maddie felt an enormous sense of failure, the bullying having done its job of knocking the edges off her, and so she wasn't as inclined to play with her younger sister. In many ways Maddie had more to de-school from – but in those early days she walked around in something of a daze, if truth be told.*

*My biggest regret is that we didn't de-school Maddie in the same way . . . I tried to bring her to group too quickly. She was sad in the first few months because she fully expected the bullies (friends) to not want her to go or leave school – it broke our hearts.*

*I want to share a curious story. When Kiki was still at school, I was talking with her teacher about the idea of extra tutoring. I said, 'Why don't I join the lesson, because I've always struggled with maths myself? That way Kiki could* see that learning can happen at any age . . .' The teacher looked at me utterly gobsmacked and said, 'No No No No! It wouldn't be good for her to know that YOU'VE struggled with maths, because she can see that you're successful.' The inference here was that the teacher didn't want Kiki to think that there was any other option than knowing maths. It seems to be the business model of private schools (and the school system at large) that everything needs to be learnt in one way in order for life to be lived successfully and meaningfully.

The teacher was essentially horrified! God forbid that anyone could make a success of themselves without being able to do maths . . . We must not promote such an idea to our children. I was left feeling a bit embarrassed, if I'm honest, and even found myself apologising for making such a foolish suggestion. This, incidentally, is one of the negatives of not having a formal education. I can easily feel shame about not having O Levels; it's taken me all these years to get to a place where I don't have this hang-up anymore and it feels so good! Even now, when the girls encounter academic snobbery in others, I really encourage them to own their alternative lifestyle and education.

## Mark

When Maddie came out of school, Nadia really wanted her to have an equivalent amount of time to decompress and de-school. *Unfortunately, what felt like the right decision for Kiki didn't (at first) feel like the right decision for Maddie. She was hurtling towards the need to take GCSEs, and, in a different way, once again on the horizon was yet another worrying deadline. Whereas we had the luxury of time with Kiki to soften the edges of learning and gently move her through subjects – I quite quickly got locked into thinking we needed to get Maddie shipshape for some sort of GCSE action in a few years' time.*

*My attitude to GCSEs and Maddie is perhaps where I've personally encountered the most stress around home-schooling. The stress never came from the subjects we were learning, or how to teach her, or how to make them interesting. The stress came from the over-arching question of when or if she was going to take the exams. It would be fair to say that I have wobbled back and forth on this topic all the way through. She is now seventeen and considering going to the Guildhall or some other performing arts college to pursue her passions (music and acting). Looking back at Maddie and my constant lack of confidence around the GCSE issue, my one regret is that I didn't boldly make the decision that I (and Maddie) have happily settled on now. It transpires that in order to pursue the career Maddie most wants (singing, song-writing and acting) the most basic requirements are literacy (functional English skills), which she has had since a very young age, and basic numeracy (or, as we call it, 'maths for life'). I wish I'd had the courage of my convictions when setting out on Maddie's* learning odyssey to trust that it would be okay if she didn't necessarily take any GCSEs. I hesitate even as I write this sentence, for fear of what people might say or the judgements they might make – but what I have discovered over the years is that this fear or worry is a hangover from my own deeply ingrained prejudices that were formed through my experience of education.

I wish I had been bolder and more certain in the plan that I ended up pursuing, rather than always feeling like I needed to straddle the needs (and judgements) of the system versus the needs of my daughter.

What I have essentially tried to do over the years is parallel some of the recommended subjects and topics within the national curriculum – but doing them all in our own way.

I took personal responsibility for subjects such as history, English literature, history of art, geography and film studies. I would use the textbooks and syllabuses of these subjects to provide a skeleton-plan of what we needed to cover – with the freedom to go off-piste and really delve deeper into those subjects that made Maddie's heart sing.

I would constantly oscillate between feeling Maddie absolutely needed to take GCSEs in order to comply with the norm, and there being no need for her to be tested on knowledge or learning that was clearly expanding her mind and her heart. At times this oscillating has been truly torturous. GCSEs are the crack cocaine of the educational establishment. They're a tough habit to kick.

## Nadia

*I come from a family where everybody is successful and only two of them have O Levels. I was brought up by parents who never held much store by qualifications. We were encouraged to make our hobbies our careers.*

*My father would often say, 'Try to avoid having a boss. Be your own boss.' Ha ha ha! There aren't many fathers who would encourage their kids to be freelancers, with all the financial insecurity that comes with that. But he made the life of a freelancer sound . . . well . . . like a life of freedom. I remember being horrified at the thought of losing my 'freedom' years ago when I was offered a two-year contract to present the BBC's The One Show. I turned it down. I like being my own boss. I suppose I feel the same about my girls.*

*So, the entire concept of GCSEs and qualifications for my kids was a curious one for me. I've never admitted this to anyone, but if I'm really honest, when other parents tell me about their hopes and dreams for their children's GCSEs or their children's actual GCSE marks I will give forced 'wows' and 'whoop's and say what I'm supposed to say (recognising, of course, that the kids had worked bloody hard to get them). But I have always been left cold by the meaning of them. For me any number of GCSES will tell me nothing about the person – it will only tell me they got a GCSE . . .*

*Throughout my adult life, I've wondered whether I should have gone the more conventional route – there have been times when I've thought I should have ticked all the boxes.*

But as I've got older I've realised that it's the word should that sticks out the most. Why do I think in these terms? Where is the pressure to conform coming from, when I am a happy and successful person? But when I look back at these shoulds and examine these doubts more, what I realise is that I'm wondering whether I could have paid more attention to educating myself as a person, because this simply doesn't need to be measured in terms of qualifications. So, turning to the subject of my children and GCSEs, I know this is an awful thing to say, but I've never felt in my heart that this was where Maddie needed to go. Ever since day dot she has wanted to be a performer. Her college choices offer places based on extracurricular activities, auditions and face-to-face interviews. The need for GCSEs simply isn't there for Maddie in the way that is for many other children – and given we had the ability to educate her up to the level of GCSEs, we ultimately decided to give her the choice of taking them or not. Looking at her own passions, her career path and the college requirements, she elected not to. I believe she has benefitted from a natural education that has set her on a path to making her hobby into her career.

For instance, she is the only child I've ever spoken to who loves Shakespeare! I'm convinced this is because she never had to sit through it at school! Don't get me wrong: I want her to be well educated, I want her to always be open to learning new things, I want her to be hungry for knowledge and open to many differing opinions. I want her to have an A* in emotional intelligence (a very valuable commodity in *a world soon to be run by robots!!). I want her to be exposed to many different things that could potentially make her heart sing. I just don't believe an A\* in a GCSE will mean that she has achieved all these things.*

*I know for Mark, the question 'To GCSE or Not to GCSE?' was particularly thorny. Mark was hell-bent for many years on keeping the girls close to the GCSE syllabuses of various subjects such as history and English literature, but he was forever tearing his hair out with how unimaginative and inflexible the curriculum was. Mark (the graduate) was feeling that the GCSEs in the very subjects he adored were not going to fire up Maddie's imagination in the way he had hoped they would.*

*I went along with the dream because I knew Mark was so worried, and because - who knows? - he may have been right. But in my heart of hearts I knew that wasn't Maddie's path, and so did Mark . . .*

## Mark

*Only in the past year or so have I truly felt comfortable with Maddie's decision not to pursue GCSEs. For me, it is infinitely more important that she hits eighteen with a belief that learning doesn't suddenly stop at the end of GCSEs, A Levels or a degree. Yes, she needs to think about her career and the ways in which she will pursue her creative profession - but I know that as she enters the world she has a genuine love* and understanding of the things she has studied rather than a sense that she simply needed to know them in order to regurgitate the right answers in order to get the right grades. When I think of the girls and their learning journey, I often find myself thinking about the fable of the Tortoise and the Hare. Many people understand what we are doing in terms of giving Maddie and Kiki the chance to 'be the tortoise' – in other words to win the race by taking their time to get round the course. But for me and, by extension, the girls, I can't help thinking that perhaps there is no actual race to be won. Maybe there isn't a finishing line – and neither should there be. What if the point of life is to continually keep running, to continually keep learning, and to continually be the tortoise? As we have said to both Kiki and Maddie through-out their learning, if a qualification is needed or might prove helpful as a gateway to something else then we will always explore the possibility of taking it. Given Maddie's passion for the performing arts and knowing that she could always win a place at college based on an audition and her busy extra-curricular life, it has felt okay to allow Maddie to continue learning without going through the potentially demotivating process of taking an exam and failing. With Kiki things could well be different . . .

# The mystic arts of homeschooling

*You can be creative in anything: in maths, science, engineering, philosophy as much as you can in music or in painting or in dance.*

Sir Ken Robinson

One of the most daunting aspects of homeschooling is the sense that there are countless academic subjects out there, all of which we as parents and teachers will somehow need to become expert in. STOP!!

One of the worst things we can do as parents in general, and as homeschoolers specifically, is panic. If you can, try and remove the pressure of time and the pressure of scope (when it comes to the school curriculum) entirely from your mind. This takes a certain amount of deprogramming, which is *not* easy.

Remind yourself that you're *not* a teacher. You are a *facilitator*. You are going to be learning alongside your child. This is a crucial distinction. We underestimate the ways in which we can inadvertently quiz kids on their knowledge in the simplest of situations. Sometimes, a request as benign as 'Tell me what you learnt today', can spin the nervous child into a tailspin. It's a mini exam. They're put on the spot. Blind panic ensues. Therefore, it's important to find ways of not *testing* your child's knowledge, but rather helping them to feel like they're acquiring knowledge *alongside* you. If the girls ask us a question and we don't know what the answer is (which happens a lot) we will invariably say, 'Let's find out!' or 'See if we can find out!'. Children visibly relax when adults admit they don't know something. As Maddie once said, the problem she had with the 'bad' teachers she encountered was that they all seemed to start from the premise that half the kids in the class were stupid.

Remind yourself that you don't have to teach your kids on your *own*. You *don't* have to teach them *everything*. There are groups out there, classes out there, there are countless teachers and tutors out there; if you're lucky, you will have relatives and friends who will prove useful, you even now have *this* book in your hand (ha ha). Everything doesn't have to happen *now*, or *tomorrow* or *next week*. Contrary to what the government and the press would have us think, there *is* time.

## The different types of homeschooling

When we first considered the homeschooling choices ahead of us for each of our girls (which were very different for both of them given the difference in their ages), things felt insurmountable. It's very easy to feel that as a homeschooling parent you will be somehow expected to do the job of an *entire* school. You don't, and you won't! Again, it's a matter of deprogramming yourselves.

However, what was quite an eye opener to both of us at the beginning was the many ways in which homeschooling can be done. Just as there are different types of school, so too are there different ways to homeschool your children. If there's one thing we'd like to be able to do, it's turn back the clocks and have someone remind us that it's okay to find it difficult to choose an approach. This was possibly the one area in which we both didn't quite agree with each other's visions or instincts about what was right for our girls. Firstly, let's list the different flavours of homeschooling:

### Homeschool pick 'n' mix

If you're not in a position to take your children out of school, and yet you'd really like to, we really believe that you can pick 'n' mix from all the different kinds of homeschooling techniques out there. In this way, some of these alternative strategies can be used in a complementary fashion to run alongside the more conventional schooling they are already receiving.

Learning isn't only about learning 'stuff'. Learning can – and should – be *fun*. Learning is life changing. Learning isn't a dirty word, and sadly most kids in school find the learning word nothing other than a promise to find things difficult. To learn shouldn't be about struggling.

1. There's the kind of homeschooling that is very formal. The children get up at a set time every day, some wear uniforms, they have a blackboard, follow the curriculum, and generally replicate the same schedule as they would have followed in school. In this model, the homeschooler tries to recreate both the conditions and structures of school in a domestic setting, utilising set texts, the national curriculum and following the set syllabus for various subjects. This is the type of homeschooling that most of the developed world tried to enact during the recent coronavirus lockdown. (The idea being that the child keeps focused and has a clear sense of when and what they are doing.)

2. There's the flexi-learner who often does a three- or four-day week at school and spends the other days in a home-schooling setting, so they effectively straddle both worlds. In many ways, this is a bit like being an adult taking a part-time course that slots into the rest of their lives. Admittedly there aren't many schools that allow for this flexibility, but we have come across a few kids who learnt in this way. It's analogous to seventeen and eighteen year olds mixing and matching their learning between different further education institutions.

3. Then there's child-led learning. This is all about the child dictating the subjects, the interests, the pace at which a subject is explored and the nature of the work done as a consequence. This is about allowing your child the freedom to gain first-hand experience of a subject, idea or activity and then giving them the time, space and creative freedom to explore it as they see fit. This can be quite nerve-wracking, because of course there's the fear they may just hit a block right at the beginning. That's where we as parents step in as facilitators, finding ways to nudge their enquiries further.

4. Then there's radical unschooling, which is a variant of child-led learning. This is the type of homeschooling the media loves. This is where all bets are off. Rules are hurled in the bin. Children are trusted to intuit and decide many of the things that are best for them. This undoubtedly

includes not steering their learning, but can also include the ways in which they socialise, what and when they eat, when they go to bed. This is about allowing your children to follow their own rhythm rather than a schedule. This is about querying the very concept of how learning is chopped up into digestible subjects and then repackaged as knowledge. This is about as holistic and – to the mainstream world – as anarchic as homeschooling can get. Check out the movie *Captain Fantastic* to see it in action. The basic idea here is that children are naturally curious and will eventually find their own way to everything that will fire them up and make their hearts sing if left to their own devices. You can see why it's called radical – it's pretty damn radical.

## Nadia

*Personally, I couldn't think of anything worse than recreating a school environment at home. All the restrictions of a formal education with none of the friends or activities. More often than not, this type of schooling is enacted by families of faith for whom there is a feeling that the system is not tolerant of their belief systems. I remember in the early days one homeschool mother saying to me, 'Traditionally the ONLY people who were homeschoolers were religious zealots, nutters or ex-teachers. Nowadays all types are doing it!'*

*When the coronavirus crisis descended upon us all, I felt*

*so sorry for all those families suddenly plummeted into recreating school at home. I felt the nation was forced into a ludicrous situation. Parents stressed and worried about everything in their lives, now being asked to recreate school in their homes while simultaneously trying to maintain continuity with their work commitments. Utterly ridiculous.*

*If I had been in charge I would have said, 'Take this time to rest, chill, take a breather, enjoy, play and reconnect with your children.' When else have we ever - culturally - been given the chance to just be with our kids in a guilt-free fashion? I would have urged the nation to use this time to get to know their kids better. Discover what truly makes their hearts sing. I would have repeatedly eased parents minds and hearts by reassuring them that their children's lives were not going to be ruined by missing a few months of school, but that in fact their lives could be enriched by having time and space to reflect on life. I would have encouraged parents to allow their kids to get bored (God forbid!). In all seriousness, boredom is a crucial part of becoming creative, and yet we live in pathological fear of ever letting our kids get bored. I personally think it's a travesty that children aren't allowed to get bored anymore. If they're not being driven by the ever-mounting demands of an increasingly neurotic educational system, they spend even more of their time outside school at more and more after-school clubs. In fact, Mark and I would sometimes argue about the fact that he would never let them get bored when they were little. He always wanted them to be doing something or learning something or experiencing something. Which of course was great in one way, but in another can generate stress.*

*Interestingly, when we first went into lockdown, within just a matter of a few days, many of my friends complained about their kids constantly saying they were bored. I can honestly say we haven't heard the girls say they are bored for years. They always seem to have some musical, acting or art project going on their rooms - either that or (contrary to what most people think about homeschooling) they are invariably socialising via the technology on their phones and their laptops. I have to say that I feel blessed to think that both our girls are real self-starters when it comes to occupying their time outside of learning.*

## Mark

*When looking at the many different ways in which you can homeschool your kids, I find myself getting frustrated with the definitions. For me, I have come very slowly to an acceptance that the best way to teach your kids, or facilitate their learning, is to simply go with the flow. It's a little like riding a thoroughbred bareback (which I've only ever done once to be fair - and badly at that). Over time, I've come to realise that we have adopted and adapted bits and pieces from every different approach to homeschooling. I have always felt it important to use the backbone of the national curriculum as a measuring stick against which to either enter a subject* more deeply, or to seriously consider whether we need to step towards it at all.

For example, the subject of reading and literature. I have done comprehension with the girls throughout their learning - but I have also encouraged them both to read all the recommended set texts as well as more books beyond them.

Kiki has read Animal Farm, The Curious Incident of the Dog in the Night-time, Lord of the Flies, 1984, and will read much more beyond what is recommended. Maddie was reading A-Level English texts ahead of her years, not in order to take A Levels, but in order to write songs inspired by these texts. She has written songs about The Crucible, The Great Gatsby, All the Birds Singing and has even moved on to books such as American Psycho as well as the movie Joker - which she has used as springboards to writing and performing songs that explore the themes emerging out of these books and films.

I know for a fact that forcing Maddie to write essays about each book would have killed stone dead how she read them and what she got from them. She would have approached reading the book as an onerous task. But suggesting she translated the ideas, themes, characters, mood and messages of these books through the medium of song-writing and performance was a different way of encouraging her to dig deep into the novels and stories, to really allow what spoke to her most in the book to float to the surface. I would argue that by removing the idea that her appreciation of a book could be 'wrong' or 'right', we have created the space for her to understand and enjoy it much more deeply. She often exclaims, 'Dad - all my friends are taking countless GCSEs but none of them have read as much as me!'

This approach is a fusion of child-led learning, radical unschooling and syllabus-based homeschooling. I think we can easily get hung up on the definitions of how we teach or how we learn, when in matter of fact true learning is a very hard thing to measure or calculate.

## Dealing with opposition

Sometimes, when talking to people about the reasons behind why we decided to homeschool, we are met with resistance, scepticism, and, if we are honest, a strange hostility. It's taken us many years to work out why this is. We are all (Mark especially) taught to accept that there is essentially *one* way to learn. There is a *fixed* sense of structure, a relatively fixed syllabus and curriculum and the entire system essentially needs to follow this template. It doesn't take a genius to come to the conclusion that if you push countless young creative minds through what is essentially a huge system, you are going to produce a certain level of conformity when it comes to what is learnt, how it is learnt and why it is learnt. Each part of the education system is designed and structured to slot into the subsequent part of the equation. It doesn't really allow for creative distraction, exploration, deviation or change. It's a little like preparing for an enormous ski-jump. Each part of the training is inexorably leading to the moment when you will jump, and hopefully land in a destination that you pretty much decided on at a much younger age.

The reason we experience quite a bit of pushback is because to swim against the current is potentially very threatening. There is also, without a shadow of doubt, that very British sentiment of 'What makes YOU so special?' when it comes to children in any way following their dreams or more esoteric passions. Indeed, it's one of the main reasons we describe ourselves as such American-ophiles: we love the way it seems to be part of the culture to think *anything* and *everything* is possible.

The vast majority of families, institutions and businesses have a vested interest in the system working in the way that it does. It is streamlined. It is manageable. It allows the economy to run smoothly; and *yes*, it does allow for *all* these things!! But, as a parent, surely it is our God-given right to question this received wisdom – or this received system – especially if we feel it is NOT serving our children effectively or meaningfully?

## The 'S' word

When opposition to the idea of homeschooling begins to run out of steam – the last hurrah tends to gravitate towards the idea of socialising. The idea being that if you don't go to school you will become socially isolated and inept, never getting used to the cut and thrust of social interaction.

The 'S' word, as we call it; 'But what about socialising?' is usually considered to be the trump card when kicking homeschooling or any form of alternative learning into the long grass. But it's important to remember that just because children are surrounded by lots of other children all day, doesn't mean that the socialising is always positive. In fact, when Maddie read *Lord of the Flies* it resonated with her as an apt metaphor of the ways in which schooling and the class system can socialise in an entirely dysfunctional manner. What seems 'socialised' to one person, can easily seem like bare-faced prejudice to another.

From the get-go, we need to stress that homeschooling

can be as social or unsociable as you want it to be. Naturally there are times during one-to-one learning when your child will not be alongside classmates. But (and it's a big but) other kids can often be a distraction, the number of kids can dilute the learning, and if they don't fit in a child can feel as alone in a class as a child who is literally on their own. Outside of one-to-one learning situations, most homeschooled kids belong to countless groups, social clubs or learning hubs. The advantage of many of these groups is that there are no strict limits on ages and so peer-groups are not strictly age-limited the way they are in school. Over the years Kiki has developed friendships with other kids older than her and Maddie has developed friends younger than her.

In many ways, just as school compartmentalises learning into bitesize chunks, so it does exactly the same with socialising. Whether it be your year, form or tutor group, or the ability stream you're in, school often dictates and controls our kids' social choices. So the idea that school is the *only* place children can learn how to socialise is worth questioning.

Don't get us wrong, to keep your child socially active as a homeschooler is very demanding. You need to put in the legwork, keep pushing and keep trying. But the prospect of your child discovering like-minded friends makes it worth it.

> *Public schools were not only created in the interests of industrialism – they were created in the image of industrialism. In many ways they reflect the factory culture they were designed to support.*
>
> Sir Ken Robinson, *The Element*

## Nadia

*I can definitely say that I have worked very hard at the 'S' word for my girls. Socialising has always been a big worry for me about homeschooling, as I know only too well how important it is for us humans to have our own tribes. I also recognise that it's vital for our children to test their behaviour and problem-solving skills around other kids – and that in many ways school can offer the best approximation of 'life in the big bad world'. But we were faced with impossible choices regarding the ways in which our kids were being treated at school. Bullying (as in Maddie's case) is one of the most common reasons for many parents to decide to homeschool. So, before you say, 'Kids only learn how to socialise in the big bad world by going to school and having the sides knocked off them', I urge you to hold back your judgement until you have actually had first-hand experience of bullying.*

*In fact, at the beginning of our homeschooling journey, I think I drove the kids a bit crazy taking them to every group imaginable, forging friendships with mums of children the same age as our girls in order to make sure they were exposed to the right peer group. This could be very draining, because although I loved some of the parents, their kids were absolute nightmares, while there were some parents who were a pain in the neck, but their kids were joyful. In other words, it was just like school. I found the whole thing utterly exhausting in the early days, and felt like I had a constant migraine from grinning at every parent and every child in every single situation I entered, just in case there happened to be a perfect friend for either one of our girls. I worried almost constantly about the 'S' word, and discovered that even outside the school system, kids can still be horrid to each other.*

*As a homeschooler, you are with your children most of the time, so you can't help but see (in close up) how children treat each other, and it ain't always pretty. Honestly, when we leave our children at the school gate, we have no idea what is really going on in the school day for our kids. As a homeschooler, there's the joy of seeing everything, but then there's also the horror, too: it's a double-edged sword.*

*So, in response to the idea that your kids can only have the edges knocked off them in the school environment, I can testify for the fact that it happens in the homeschooling world too!*

*I also had the added problem that Kiki hadn't really forged any close friendships in her time at school, so she didn't* want to hang out with any of her old friends and had to try and make an entirely new set of mates – not the easiest thing to do when you are very shy. It's safe to say she had some real highs and lows with this.

I think we also battled with the fact that there was a fair amount of suspicion towards me from many parents, simply because I was 'off the telly'. I understood why, the mainstream press love to portray the homeschool community in a very poor light, and some of the people I met had been sorely bitten by this. There is a huge stigma created by the mainstream media about anyone trying to do anything differently. I had encountered the same issues surrounding my choice to have home births, too. People can be unduly suspicious of others who choose an alternative route – they see it as a threat. It really is quite eye-opening to discover how conservative (with a small c) some of the even the most progressive people can be when confronted with the subject of homeschooling.

## Mark

It always struck me that there were in fact more opportunities to socialise and mix with other kids (and young adults) of all ages within the homeschooling world. Because the same rules don't apply, there is a fluidity to the types and ages of people our children can meet. Kiki has always naturally gravitated to kids slightly older than her. Her tastes are that bit older, and she feels more comfortable when she's the younger of the group. This is something that's quite hard to do within the conventional schooling system.

Every day of the week, me and Nadia would be taking the girls to drama classes, trying to get them into sports activities, they would always be going to this or that dance class – and of course there were always countless sleepovers. Homeschooled kids have a lot more sleepovers than other kids, because they're not having to get up at some arbitrary early time to be at a desk or ready for assembly! I must admit I found this part of it all the most challenging. But it really isn't true to suggest that one of the main reasons not to homeschool is because your kids will miss out on socialising. You and your kids will be able to socialise as much or as little as you please – but the bonus with homeschooling is that you and your child will have a bigger pool of people to choose from. You won't be limited by the kids in your child's tutor group.

Where we have encountered issues around socialising has had nothing to do with homeschooling itself – it's only ever been to do with the confidence of our girls in any given situation. I genuinely believe that any issues you may have around your children and socialising has nothing to do with the type of education they're receiving, it's far more to do with the individual circumstances and character of your child. As Nadia says, if you have a shy or nervy child who struggles to socialise, they will undoubtedly get lost in a school scenario, they will run the risk of being marginalised and *bullied. The benefits of homeschooling aren't that the same might not happen - of course it might. But you are much closer to witnessing it, and so you can take action or help them through it without all the stress of having to go through the usually ineffective manoeuvres of approaching the head and proving what's going on.*

## The limits of conventional learning

But there is another side to the 'S' word. As well as the socialising side of things (friendships, etc.), there is also the concept of settling into a social understanding of the world, and as we have discovered on our own journey, what the syllabus and curriculum teaches children is never the entire story. The Black Lives Matter movement, fired up recently by the tragic death of George Floyd, has been an enormously important part of day-to-day life in our household, and what has emerged from the controversy and the civil rights movement afterwards has been a realisation that the history we are taught and told about isn't the only history to be told. Through listening to music and watching documentaries, the footage on social media (horror of horrors) that the mainstream broadcasters won't show, as well as movies (such as *BlacKKKlansman, Just Mercy, Queen & Slim* and *The Hate U Give*) both our girls have come to discover that there are often glaring omissions in the stuff that the system deems to be teachable.

For instance, in our teaching of the Irish Question (the history of the troubles in Northern Ireland) it was important for us to fully describe the conflict from both sides of the religious divide. Explaining (by also using the parallels of Palestine and Apartheid in South Africa) that one person's terrorist group can be another group's freedom fighter.

## Mark

*I often say to the girls that learning isn't just about learning things such as dates, facts and formulas; learning is about knowing how to make yourself open to more learning. I worry that we are selling our kids a total pup when it comes to education. We've made the entire process a curiously stressful race to the finish. Jump this hurdle, jump that hurdle, get this grade, get that grade, and somehow this is the be all and end all of learning. Learning should never stop. Learning should never be closed off. Maddie and Kiki have often spoken of the ways in which their friends at school will learn about this or that subject in order to simply get the required grade to go to the next institution or get the correct grade that the system requires of them. All I've ever want for our girls is to know and recognise that learning doesn't stop. Learning is all about adding to who you are – and yes, for many children who find a passion for learning, the system can be a brilliant way of ensuring you reach into as many different areas as possible, but there is always more than one way to skin a rabbit.*

Politics is a big thing in our household. We are interested in it, and we talk about it a lot with the girls. We spend a lot of time talking about American politics. We've discussed all the ins and outs of Brexit. The coronavirus has been a brilliant opportunity to talk to the girls about the ways in which the media manipulate and package the news in order to gain viewers and readers.

We had a very funny instance recently where we were trying to minimise the fear levels in the house surrounding the extent to which the Covid-19 crisis felt like it was spiralling out of control. I urged the girls to always check the name of the news gatherer when reading a news story on their devices, to ratify the source of the news and ensure it's not fake. One day Maddie came home in a terrible state about some new development, and the first thing I asked was, 'Where did you read this – is it a trustworthy news outlet?' Her face dropped as she said, 'That's the thing: yes! . . . It's the Guardian!!' Bless her, I then had to reveal that even the Guardian is sometimes after the reader numbers!

A brilliant magazine that is a digest of the week's major news stories is a publication for kids and young adults called the Week – we use it as a tool to access the news and discuss things over dinner.

## Where learning happens

The other huge misapprehension about homeschooling is that it all happens around the kitchen table or in the home. In fact, although we use it, we *hate* the phrase homeschooling – a much more accurate description would be something like 'non-school-based learning'.

Every single conceivable place of interest to visit, whether it's National Trust, English Heritage, Historic Scotland, Kew Gardens, Heritage Ireland, a local museum or an RHS garden, will have worksheets and guides for kids, students and teachers on their website. If you want to provide a little more structure to the visit you can print these off and take them along. Even if you don't use this material as a means of testing your kids – have it as background for you! It means that as you go around a venue you are better equipped to explain what's going on. We've lost count of the number of exhibitions we've taken the girls to which we've visited beforehand – so that we can test how leg weary they might get before going.

We also take time to crib up on the artist and some of the techniques or reasons behind some of their most significant works. It has the double bonus of making you sound infinitely more knowledgeable – but it also means if your kids want to go deeper into the detail you can do this with them.

Holidays are the same. There is *always* the opportunity

to discuss whatever you come across and remember it doesn't matter if you don't know the answers. Find them out together!

In almost every conceivable situation there are questions you can ask your kids that you can learn the answers to together. Finding out what things are made of, how old the artist was when he made this or that work, where do we recognise this or that theatrical actor from on TV. Smartphones allow you to find out all sorts about a playwright, an artist, a building, or a bridge, even.

A game you can play is to ask something like 'Where are we?' Then start to unpack where you are. What country? What city or town or village or beach? By what sea? In what continent? What's the name of the road? Why is that the name of the road? Why is this road here? Where does it lead?

We've found some of the simplest conversations about, say, the River Thames and how it keeps the city alive, or has allowed the city to grow, really brings the girls' imaginations alive. When we explore history, we approach it like a costume drama or a film. After all, history is story-telling from the past so it lends itself well to dramatization.

## Blowing their minds

How big is the universe? Why is the sky blue? Why am I me and you you? These are all questions that children – who are naturally curious – come up with, and they will *always* react with great excitement when you admit the whole thing blows your mind as much as it does theirs, and show that you're ready to find out the answers alongside them.

One particularly important moment in Kiki's learning of prehistoric history was the realisation at quite an early point that a lot of it is based on an enormous number of well-informed guesses and assumptions drawn from remarkably few archaeological discoveries. Kiki fizzed with excitement when she began to sense that even what teachers teach us is based on the limited resources available to historians and archaeologists. Presenting the world to your kids as incomplete and full of big wonderful gaps is absolutely okay. In fact, we'd say it's important. It will allow you in later learning to encourage them to appreciate that failure, or not having *all* the answers, is an important of life and learning!

## Teaching by stealth

> *Some of the most brilliant, creative people I know did not do well at school. Many of them didn't really discover what they could do – and who they really were – until they'd left school and recovered [our emphasis] from their education.*
>
> Sir Ken Robinson

Regardless of how your kids learn, or where they learn there is one huge truism when it comes to our role as parents. In order to convince reluctant children or teens to do anything, you *have* to use a fair amount of stealth and good old-fashioned deception to get them to coop-erate. Subterfuge is a major component of homeschooling. You need to be clever, smart, deceitful and a little bit naughty. Where Mark refers to the extended family as 'The Jedi Knights of Learning', Nadia refers to this side of things as 'The Dark Side'.

No amount of simply telling your kids to do some comprehension work is going to be met with excitement or enthusiasm. In fact, we never really understood what comprehension work actually meant until we started to unpack every conceivable part of teaching our children. Comprehension is, of course, comprehending the world around you. It's about checking the ability of children to take in information or experiences, be able to understand them, draw conclusions from them and use them in other similar or dissimilar situations.

The most obvious comprehension in the book, is of . . . well . . . books! We all know the drill. Here's a passage of writing. Read it, and then answer these questions. Okay. So, some children, including the younger Mark, absolutely relish this. But for the younger Nadia, this was a cue to leap up, sing a song and show everyone her knickers.

Homeschooling is about finding different ways to achieve the same goals, and one area that has been in many ways transformational for the girls has been the way in which Mark did something unique with their love of films.

## Mark

*About two years ago, when Nadia and I started to discuss the ways in which we could link our professional skillset to new and emerging technologies, we decided it would make sense to put some effort into our YouTube channel. We had launched the channel many years earlier to showcase a really sweet film of Kiki (then seven) being introduced to her brand-new puppy Chi Chi. Ben, my eldest daughter Issy's boyfriend at the time, was a tech whiz kid and he set up a channel, but afterwards it lay dormant for years.*

*But then I hit upon an idea. I've made many films and*

documentaries for TV, I've made short films myself, I studied film, went to film school and love nothing more than talking about and analysing films (mainstream ones as well as arthouse ones). I am as comfortable with Iron Man as I am with Ingmar Bergman! However, in all the times I'd been scrolling online looking for intelligent or multi-generational reviews of new movies, I had never found a movie review channel that approached things as a family, for a family. And so, The Popcorn Junkies was born. I decided to use this movie channel as a covert means of building the girls' film comprehension. I took them to see more and more films and the deal was that afterwards we would come home, pop up a couple of cameras and talk about them.

What the girls didn't realise was that en-route to the cinema, I would be wittering on about the fact that I really wanted them to think about the story, what emotions we were supposed to feel, why, how, what did the fact that Chris Pratt was starring in the film make us think the film might be like, how was it shot, what about its use of music, listen out for your favourite song, etc. - the list could go on forever.

After the film, back at home we would record our review and upload it. We still do it to this day. Both the girls' capacity to approach a film and, more importantly, their ability to approach a fictional story has blossomed. They are always thinking of characterisation, the message of the film, the choices the director has made, the ways in which the script worked or not, the performances, etc.

The brilliant thing about testing a child's comprehension

*of a story (regardless of whether it is a film or a book) is that the skills of interrogation are entirely transferable from medium to medium. Maddie and Kiki's ability to probe the ways in which a book tells a story is always developing, whether it's the use of chapters, the first or third person, metaphors, similes, analogies or any number of other techniques, all these things are now less threatening for them to home in on and have an opinion about.*

*So, you tell me. None of these individual (often passionate) journeys to the hearts of countless films and books have been tested or put through exam conditions – does that render them redundant? I don't think so. The girls remember every single thing they've watched and every single thing they've read in such vivid detail it is sometimes frightening! They also take real ownership and pride in the films, TV series, books or graphic novels that they read and watch. They always have skin in the game rather than viewing these things as a means to a GCSE end. Nadia is intimidated by how discerning the girls can be at times.*

Obviously, there are *many* circumstances when you will find yourself trying to work with a reluctant child or moody teenager, but resistance and reluctance to learn also happens in a school environment, sometimes with catastrophic consequences. Every school has to deal with kids who aren't paying attention and are playing up or talking in class, or who bunk lessons, forget to do their homework and so on.

It's unrealistic to expect a homeschooled child to be

one hundred per cent on point throughout their learning. It's just *never* going to happen. But one of the best elements of homeschooling your children is that you build into the day some decompression time. If they don't feel like doing geography in the morning, be fluid – move it to later in the day. Or, better still, coming back to the idea of teaching by stealth – suggest they watch something that is closely aligned to what they should have been learning about. At the end of the day we are *all* allowed to have bad days, but the conventional schooling approach puts extraordinary pressure on a class of twenty to thirty different teenagers to all to be in precisely the same learning headspace at the same time. If you think about it, it's a recipe for disaster, and in both Nadia and Mark's own experiences classes often descended into chaos.

## Deal or no deal

Striking deals with your homeschooled child is a neat way to motivate them. If you trust them to go away and research a topic under their own steam – you are sort of handing them the steering wheel of their own car. Fine, it doesn't need to be done today, but let's share what you've found out over breakfast in two or three days' time. If you deliver on your side of the bargain, then yes – of course we can go to Nando's after the next visit to the Tate!!

## Screen time and technology

One of the other major worries around homeschooling is the idea that if the children are not at school, they're going to be on their phones all the time. Once again, we can't pretend we live in some homeschooling idyll where the girls go and collect hens' eggs every day and only do their schoolwork on a pad of paper. iPhones, iPads, laptops and all manner of other tech is the norm. Of course, there is the potential for any child to spend too much time on their smartphone or laptop looking at the wrong things, and this does have to be guarded against, but a cannier way to approach the issue of screen time and tech is to recognise that these devices are a brilliantly inventive way to access the world. As well as games on these devices, there are also tools for receiving news and learning. Yes, you need to have some rules in place (and believe me, we have struggled with this), but these are ubiquitous problems for parents and their kids in the twenty-first century.

Don't forget – these devices also offer a brilliant way for homeschooled kids to interact with each other when they're not together in a group or a class. They allow easy access to all manner of brilliant films, documentaries, photographs and music, and something that a lot of adults fail to recognise (whether as homeschoolers or not) is the huge amount of creativity and entrepreneurial skill involved in some of the content created by a predominantly younger demographic for platforms such as YouTube, Snapchat, Instagram and even TikTok.

If you are clever and you recognise that these digital portals into other worlds are every bit as valid as reading a book, you will be more likely to gain the trust and co-operation of your children. A small example of this for us as a family, is that every weekend on our YouTube channel we make a Sunday show that involves cookery lessons, a read-through and discussion of the news headlines, a book review, but also (most importantly) a section that showcases all the things teens, tweens and young adults are finding funny online. You would be amazed at how sophisticated a lot of this content is. So, if you can, try not to be averse to technology and screen time. Obviously keep an eye on it, but remember, as well as being a possible nightmare, it can also be a brilliant companion to help you help your children. The best thing to aim for as a homeschooling parent is tolerance and acceptance of what your kids are into. Try not to dismiss, stand in judgement or simply pooh-pooh something because it feels irrelevant to you.

●

When the girls were at school, the 'pen licence' was a real status symbol. It was what every child received once they had accomplished the ability to do joined-up writing – you'd receive a fountain pen to celebrate your mastery of the cursive script.

In the run-up to this 'coming of age' moment, an awful lot of time was spent trying to make Kiki write using joined-up letters, and we believe this had a real impact on her writing. It meant she would really struggle to get her thoughts out of her head and onto paper. We are both convinced that this obsession with handwriting profoundly blocked Kiki's ability to freely express herself in her story-telling.

## Nadia

*So, one of the first things we did when she came out of school was allow her to write uncorrected on an iPad. She wrote and wrote and wrote without worrying about her punctuation . . . out of the blue she wrote an incredibly long and detailed story about a bear . . . that she wanted to carry on forever. Don't get me wrong, the pen skills thing is great for many kids, but there is a real need for flexibility around learning to write. The more Kiki wrote from the heart, the more she would write again, and as the spell-checker kicked in and corrected things, she found confidence in her writing. Similarly, Kindle offers a brilliant dictionary tool so that when she was reading a passage, she could simply click on a word and it would pop up the definition.*

*I feel we tend to get hysterical about these screen-based devices, when in matter of fact they are incredibly useful tools. Although a pen and piece of paper are two great pieces of technological kit, these days we also have a host of others at our disposal, all of which likewise require a very sophisticated set of skills.*

## The last watch

I remember one day buying Kiki a watch. A teacher at the time identified the watch on her wrist and challenged Kiki to tell the time. Kiki struggled, and then the teacher said, 'No wearing watches until you can tell the time.' Unsurprisingly, Kiki has never worn a watch since. Now, being fair to the teacher, she wasn't just being mean. I think she thought it would incentivise Kiki to learn how to tell the time. Sadly, it had the opposite effect.

*Much later on with Maddie homeschooling too we used to worry so much about the amount of time they spent on their phones and I think this came from a place of guilt because they weren't around other kids all day long.*

A big problem with being a homeschooling parent is that the children see how much time we ourselves spend on our phones (for work, etc.) We now have phone-free reading sessions. It is definitely something that must be constantly monitored, but the pros far outweigh the cons.

It important to say that over the years we have tried to avoid fighting over phone usage. Maddie tells us many kids have second phones for when their main phones are confiscated. Phone usage and screen time is a fact of life, it's about trying to be measured and realistic in your tussle with your kids. Be reasonable - and they will be reasonable back.

## Mark

I remember Issy, my eldest, had a boyfriend who was home-schooled. What she noticed about him was that he was unphased when he didn't know a lot about something - he could quite confidently find out for himself by searching online and trouble-shooting. Issy (a product of the main-stream system) was always in awe of how successfully and completely he could research things and find out answers. This makes me feel that it often gets forgotten just how much of an upside there is to the new technology and screens in our children's hands.

These devices serve a lot of very varied functions. Of course, we can all ( adults especially) fall down never-ending Instagram wormholes, but these devices also allow for moments of truly entrepreneurial invention. For example, when we went into lockdown during the coronavirus crisis, Maddie had a number of live showcase gigs arranged to meet music-industry types and reach a broader audience. In lockdown she has diversified precisely because of technology, doing weekly InstaGigs – performing half-hour sets, developing her craft and driving more listeners to her music on Spotify. She has started to earn from this, and so at an early age there is a correlation between using technology and potentially earning a living from doing something you love.

Kiki has used countless drawing tutorials to hone and perfect her drawing techniques in lockdown and has taken to creating comic character designs and is now considering starting to sell T-shirts and clothes with her designs on them. Technology must be understood in terms of these positives as well as the negatives. Yes, controlling screen-time can be difficult. But then it is just as difficult for non-homeschooled kids and their parents, too. Wasn't everyone exclaiming back in the seventies and eighties that children would become addicted to television and it would rot their brains? In every technological advance there is a potential for positive change as well as negative, and negotiating these pitfalls is no different regardless of how your child is educated.

# Our role as parents

When considering homeschooling, many people get stuck when it comes to the idea of finding a happy balance between work life and the education of their children. If you go into the concept as two working co-parents, it is a fact that either one of you or both of you will have to adjust your working lives in some way to accommodate. With homeschooling, as with everything, you cannot have your cake and eat it. Something has to give. As a family you have to accept that some sacrifices are going to be made – and time will have to be found from somewhere.

However, one of the most liberating aspects of home-schooling is that while, yes, your work life feels the squeeze, you also have the option to spread out the so-called 'school timetable'. The weekends are a great opportunity to make up for any lost time during the week. And if, like us, you freelance or can work from home (which, thanks to coronavirus may well become more widely accepted), you can also take advantage of structuring your own day around some (although probably not all) work commitments.

The long and the short of it is that hopefully, between yourself and maybe your partner, or a relative such as a grandparent, you can balance the learning time across the full seven days of the week. Also, don't forget that where schools stop for four weeks at Easter and six weeks over the summer, you can consider adding those weeks into your annual homeschooling commitment. That way you're probably going to approach the same amount of teaching time – or rather *learning* time – that your child would be getting across twelve months in a conventional school.

A lot of the practicalities around making homeschooling work necessitate us as parents to look at the ways in which we manage time differently. We need to loosen up. We need to improvise a bit. We need to be less regimented. The key to how we do this is that both of us are freelancers. We have some sense of our time commitments, but not always. We'd hesitate to say that one half of the parenting couple needs to fully sacrifice their work and therefore their income, because with where we all work and the ways in which we all work changing and modernising dramatically in the twenty-first century from one minute to the next – we may well be entering a new era in working from home that will mean no one parent will ever need to make the entire sacrifice.

The myth of homeschooling is that as a parent you will need to spend all your time with your kids. There are groups, there are clubs, there are classes, there are tutors. A really important tool is to reach out to your entire family and closest friends. Everyone has a passion or a specialism.

## Mark

*For instance, my mother (or Nanny Di as the kids call her) is a librarian by trade and also a huge art lover. Now retired, she is an eccentric old-school lesbian-feminist who is forever sharing in stories about being on marches, protesting for this or that reason, and talking about the ways in which gender politics have changed over the years. The girls are forever hearing stories of how the Women's Movement fought for equal rights and how things have changed over time as well as how some things haven't (with the #MeToo movement). In fact, the very concept of using the entire family as a learning and educative resource tool is a key part of homeschooling any child. Let's not forget the famous African saying 'It takes a village to raise a child.' There is huge wisdom in this. Everyone in a family has a skill, a passion or an area of expertise. In the early days, I used to refer to this idea of the family as a huge resource as the 'Jedi Knights* of Homeschooling'. Nadia's dad is an actor and writer by trade and is also of Bedouin descent. So, storytelling is a defining feature in his life both culturally and professionally. The girls have sat and listened to many tales of life in the Middle East, of the travails of being an out-of-work actor, and the joys of being a highly successful actor. Nanny Di has an obvious passion for books, but she would also on regular basis take both the girls out to see all the latest art exhibitions. Okay, they always ended up somewhere like Wagamamas for lunch afterwards, but this was an entire day of experiential learning that the kids could do with their gran, which didn't result in tired 'museum legs' or boring worksheets. Wherever Nanny Di didn't have the chance to take them deeply into the history of an artist or the techniques they used, I could pick up the slack of an evening with a book on the artist or going online to find out more.

Nadia would be able to show them how to cook - both the girls make the best spag bol of any kid I know - a skill that is rarely taught in schools, even though being able to cook for yourself is probably one of the most critical life skills a child can learn.

My passion for books and film mean that I would forever be looking to extend the types of things they'd read and the sorts of films they both watch. They're comfortable with a blockbuster superhero film but the South Korean film Parasite was also one of their favourites from last year.

## In praise of teachers

It's really important that you don't pretend to be a teacher. On many occasions we stop and remark on our absolute admiration for the teaching establishment. Our homeschooling journey has only been possible with the help of countless teachers of varying levels and varying expertises all stepping in at various points to help. The ability to translate complicated ideas into digestible and understandable chunks of meaningful information is no easy task. We cannot stress enough how much our stance towards the conventional education system isn't one that's critical of teachers. There are too many BRILLIANT teachers trying to achieve BRILLIANT things despite a system that is forever hampering their BRILLIANCE and the BRILLIANCE that kids could achieve.

Some people we know do work full-time while also home-schooling their kids. They fit the schooling around the edges of their working week and use those times when they're busiest for groups or online learning. An hour's tutoring can be equivalent to three maths classes – which is where replicating the timetables of schools is profoundly misguided. The point being that you don't have to find the same amount of time for a subject when the children are receiving one-to-one tuition rather than taking their chances in a busy classroom.

## Nadia

*During the first few weeks of deciding to homeschool, as has been the way for the past twenty years, I shared virtually everything with Loose Women. With hindsight, I wish I hadn't shared it that early. Because we didn't really know what we were doing, talking about it so early sort of set myself up for failure in terms of other people's opinions of what we were doing. When questions were asked of me, I didn't have the right answers. I didn't talk eloquently, and so I didn't feel I had represented us as a family properly. I was fearful of judgement. Over the years, I've been asked to go on various programmes to talk about it, but I've always found that in the asking, people always lean towards only wanting to prove how wrong we are. Showing what we do as wrong rather than even entertaining the idea that we might be doing something that was right. Everyone always wants a very quick answer to their questions about what we are doing, so that they can quickly dismiss it and not feel like their choice is wrong.*

*The majority of people I work with think I am mad for doing what I do, although I did have the most blissful couple* of years when Stacey Solomon was also homeschooling her kids – I didn't feel like such an outcast.

On a practical level, Loose Women is the dream job for homeschooling – its live, which means the filming days don't go on and on forever, and it's only a couple of days a week, which was always very manageable with the girls' groups and classes, and knowing Mark (being freelance) could plug the gaps.

We're also very blessed with my parents next door, and have found over the years that because an awful lot of our work and content creation (cookery columns, books, Mark's production company actually being in an annexe on the side of the house) occurs at home or near home, we had flexibility at all times, and we have been able to move the children's schedules around on a weekly basis. If one week was particularly busy, we would pick up history at the weekend or early evening instead of at eleven a.m. But of course there are countless other ways of finding flexibility: swapping days with other families, asking friends for lifts, leaning on other homeschoolers, using family members to fill in the gaps – just like most families do when it comes to the everyday toing and froing between home, school and extra-curricular activities in the mainstream system.

Working on a show like Loose Women is a privilege but it can also prove to be very intimidating. A bunch of smart, very opinionated women, all of whom are very passionate and focused on what we do in our lives and the ways we see the world. I was particularly upset when one of my colleagues wrote an op-ed piece about homeschooling, describing it as 'just another form of insidious control', implying that anyone who homeschooled had no respect for the 'discipline' enacted by the school system. This cut deep.

## Mark

I remember a critical point in our homeschooling journey was when one of Nadia's colleagues decided to publish an article in the paper. I felt it was a remarkably jaundiced piece from a woman who ironically (for me) typified and manifested rebellion and a total disregard for discipline. When I read it, I remember thinking, 'Here's someone else who seemingly can only see learning through one prism.' My mother was somewhat similar. It's a generational thing. What perplexed me more was that the woman who wrote it was herself a figurehead for a YOOF Culture back in the eighties that was all about breaking the rules, sticking fingers up to convention and tapping into more creative ways of seeing the world. It didn't upset me – I was more (to use a parental phrase) disappointed.

It's important in any honest description of what it's like to homeschool that we are truthful about the challenges too. It's not easy to maintain the work/homeschool balance. It can be very difficult. There have been many occasions when me and Nadia have disagreed or argued over which one of us needs to make this or that work sacrifice in order to pick things up with the kids. But I remember identical issues when

*I was a young parent with Issy, having the same tussles between me and her mum over which one of us should collect her from nursery. The division of labour between parents isn't easy to navigate at the best of times, and homeschooling is no exception. While you may not want to have a rigid timetable for your kids, you may well need to have a pretty strict schedule for yourselves as adults. Sometimes it takes a lot of backroom activity to provide the free, non-stressful environment required for something as unstructured as de-schooling. But, heh, that's what parents do. It's in the job description.*

## Nadia

*People often challenge me with questions such as, 'What do you do about all the things you don't know about?', 'How do you know your child wouldn't love physics?', 'What about team sports?', 'What about school trips?' (I'm sure some people question my intelligence, mistakenly assuming I am personally and single-handedly responsible for teaching them everything they know.) 'What if they will NEED their GCSEs?', 'What about competitiveness?', 'How are they going to get up in the morning?'*

## Mark

*Some of these questions are really tough to answer, which is why I would always reply by saying you need to know your child. We are all making educated guesses about our kids, whether they go to school or not. A child who might like physics could have their passion quashed by a bad physics teacher. I have heard many kids who are good at English describe the ways in which their specific teacher made the subject the most boring thing in the world to learn. Questions are very easy to ask, but more often than not, precisely the same questions can be asked of children in school. If a child has a passion for anything, they will naturally gravitate towards it, and so as a homeschooler you will become aware that your child would probably like science clubs and science lessons.*

*It's easy to find a subject that a homeschooling child isn't interested in and suggest that perhaps that could be the thing they'd have loved if they went to school. The point about homeschooling is that there is no rush to find the subjects that excite them. Team sports may well be a great thing for some kids, but just as many hate them and resent the fact that they had to do them for most of their lives. Competition is good so long as it doesn't only reward the winners. Once again, sports clubs and societies are everywhere and invariably they all happen outside school hours. Kiki has a passion for running, a solitary but still competitive sport. School trips may well be something they don't* do, but as a family we have travelled the world with our girls. Plus, as many teacher friends testify, the logistics of getting sixty-plus schoolchildren anywhere in the world (or just in the UK) and making sure they don't get lost, can make school trips so very much less efficient and infinitely more stressful than just taking a couple of children to a gallery or museum. The one-to-one discussions in smaller groups can be so much more meaningful than an enormous gang of thirty kids all daring each other to laugh at everything and take nothing seriously. A major feature of our homeschooling life is that we constantly do what we call, 'audits' on whether the ambitions of our girls may require a qualification or a GCSE. We have always reminded Maddie especially, that there are countless ways to take this or that GCSE in your own time under your own speed if you were ever to need one.

## Why do we actually have children?

One of the most unexpected, profound and existential questions that arises from homeschooling your children goes to the very heart of being a parent. Why do we have children in the first place? It may sound like a simple little question, but it isn't. We all *think* we know why we have kids – after all, between us we have four beautiful girls and we could never imagine life without them. But why do we actually have children? It's an important question to ask, because in many ways the answers we give or can't give go some way to explaining our attitudes towards education.

Yes, it's about the continuation of the human race. Yes, it's what happens between loving couples, and yes, it can happen accidentally. It's one of those questions that, as a parent, is surprisingly difficult to answer. Life is incredibly volatile, it's incredibly unpredictable, it's littered with obstacles, it's challenging, it's exciting – it's all these things and more. But why do we have children? Do we have them to try and show them a route through life that is better than our own? Do we want children to benefit from the lessons we've learnt, the affluence we've acquired? Is it an egotistical decision? Do we have children because in many ways they help to fill a void in our lives? They give us purpose. They give us a reason to be alive.

Having a child is all these things and none of these things. Having a child is beautiful and amazing and miraculous, for sure. So why isn't the way our children are educated every bit as important to us all as the very concept of having them? Why do we often end up deciding what it is we want our children to be very early in their lives?

The really difficult realisation that we've had to arrive at is that having a child is partly about showing off. Are we trying to fix the wrongs in ourselves? Do they come with all the other status symbols – showing off what our children can become, what their promise is? How much of this is about how it reflects on us as parents? Are children a second chance for us to achieve the things we weren't able to accomplish ourselves? Are our kids' achievements about their happiness or our ambitions? How often are we actually altruistic about our kids? How often when we say we are doing this or that for our child (sending to boarding school, etc.) are we actually doing it for them?

We can say this because we actually have experienced it – these ideas were precisely what informed our decision to send them to private school. When we say we want the best for our kids, what 'best' are we referring to? Is it about what looks best to other people? How many of our parenting decisions are actually about peer pressure from other parents? After all, we are all only adult children trying to parent children!!

At the end of the day, if your kid achieves everything you hoped they would, but they aren't happy – what then? Was it all meaningless?

It's our belief that *every* parent should have the freedom to educate their children in whatever way *best* suits the needs of that child. We are not *anti* any form of learning, but we are *anti* forcing all children to do it this way or that way. In writing this book we aren't for a minute promoting the idea that *everyone* should homeschool their kids – that would be an entirely inappropriate and imprac- tical suggestion. But what we do want to do is puncture the myths surrounding homeschooling and *also*, more importantly, shake up our attitudes to teaching and learning. Most importantly, we want to encourage people to realise that it is an entirely viable option.

Whenever a parent with a child at school feels things are going wrong, we often point the finger at the school. This is very much what we did after the trauma of Kiki's experience at one school and Maddie's experience at two schools. But what we have come to realise with time is that we were the ones who made the mistake of wanting an inappropriate (not inadequate) system to educate our children.

What we want this blow-by-blow account of our journey to do is kick up the dust for all parents. If we want to help our kids in life, we need to adopt a more fluid approach to learning – we need to see learning in terms of our child's happiness not just their 'academic success'. It's a truism that a happy child is more likely to learn and remember something than an unhappy and stressed child. We need to transform our educational system – and if we can't do it by changing the law, we can do it by operating on the fringes of the law. As our man-crush Sir Ken Robinson says, 'Given the challenges we face, education doesn't need to be *reformed* . . . it needs to be transformed.'

Ask yourself a simple question. How much of what you want for your children, is actually what you want for yourself? Deep down, are we *all* pushy parents?!

## What *are* the markers of success?

It's funny, because when we discussed the need for a section on success, we sort of laughed and then got a little bit intimidated. The very use of the word 'success' is diametrically opposed to our entire concept of home-schooling.

As far as we're concerned, we've always wanted our girls' education to rub up against as many things as possible – whether they are on the national curriculum or not. The central tenets of what most children *should* learn is a great spinal column for learning, and is some-thing we've pivoted around throughout both Kiki and Maddie's education. Yes, the national curriculum encourages the study of the civil rights movement at GCSE level, but a school setting would not have allowed for the 360-degree approach we took to the subject. We not only embraced the history books (exploring the events and the speeches, charting the origins of slavery, distinguishing between Martin Luther King and Malcom X), but because Maddie's passion is music we also did some really detailed and focused work on the Nina Simone song 'Strange Fruit'. We got Maddie to write about the song from the perspective of the lyncher as well as the family of the lynched boys. We listened to a radio documentary about the origins of the song and where it came from. Maddie then (being a singer) chal-lenged herself to add the song to her repertoire and has often performed it live. We encouraged a deeper sense and understanding of jazz and blues music – steering the subject matter directly towards areas of excitement and engagement that we knew would snag the girls' interests. Kiki is ardently passionate about the Netflix series *When They See Us*, which tells the story of the Central Park 5. She watched the series and we then explored and learned around the news story, watching films such as *Detroit* and *12 Years a Slave*. We also found that films with less of a direct historical angle were critical to helping the girls understand the experience of African Americans in contemporary America – so films such as *Get Out*, *Us*, *The Hate U Give* and *Queen & Slim* have all helped broaden their understanding of the civil rights movement beyond simply remembering facts and dates. They have come to understand the emotion behind the history, not simply the textbook details. For us, this experience of the civil rights topic has proved successful. But there is no GCSE at the end of it. There is no grade. There is no sense of success or failure for the girls. Like the layers of an onion, we hope it has formed an outer sense of things for them, which will subsequently equip them with a multi-layered, more rounded comprehension of the subject. History is one of those subjects that truly benefits from going 'off the grid', so-to-speak. If, as we're discovering with the Black Lives Matter movement, there are multiple untold stories to hear and legacies to be re-examined and re-explored from different perspectives, then it doesn't require a huge stretch of imagination to accept that there are multiple different ways to teach these histories.

No syllabus is sacrosanct, and no syllabus should be left unchallenged. We genuinely feel that the system struggles to unlock the inherent intelligence and creativity of *many* children simply because it tries just *one* way to access it.

To suggest that there is a *fixed measure* of success to homeschooling would be entirely contradictory. The very word 'success' presupposes an end point. A marker of accomplishment. A finishing line. A grade. What we have tried, and are still trying to teach the girls is to remain open *at all times* to learning and interpreting the world around them.

There *is no end point* to learning – and there should *never* be.

Sometimes finding stuff out or learning things isn't just about being able to remember the facts. It can also be about learning *how* to find things out in the first place. For example, every time we go to a gallery the girls will always find out what materials have been used in the works of art, they'll discover the age at which the artist created the works – and they do this as a matter of routine to amplify the experience and make their enjoyment more meaningful. This may be short-term information, but it also demonstrates an ability to enquire.

So, when we talk about children being successful – what

do we actually mean? It's an uncomfortable question. How much of the answer is about us the parents? How much of it is about our expectations for our kids rather than what is *right* for our kids?

Do we mean setting them up for life in a job to give them the money to have the things we are all supposed to want, regardless as to whether they are happy? Why does not wanting to do a job for someone else mean not wanting to work? A friend told us about a boy who just drew and drew. His parents wanted him to be a doctor and saw no value in what he did – is this the parents' fault? Or did the parents simply not know anything different because we are all so brainwashed into things?

When we have dreams for our children why is it almost a dirty thought that you just want your child to be happy? People look at you like you're sad. Does every child actually have to have an ambition – or more importantly a *permitted* ambition – there are huge rules and regulations around types of work, and the creative arts are always at the wrong end of the spectrum . . .

Is how successful we want our kids to be more about how successful we want our conversations to be with the other parents in our own peer groups? The look of total disbelief or like we are talking another language when we tell people how we have educated our girls and not pressurised Maddie into GCSEs is proof that what we are doing flies against the norm.

Who *is* the most successful mum in the playground – is it the mum whose child has every grade and success, or the mum whose kid is happiest in play and self-expression? Are you the mum standing in the playground desperately trying to prove that your kid is the best at swimming galas? Have you ever stopped and asked if this is what you or your child wants? What *are* the markers of success? We've talked a lot about how stressed our children are by the current education system, but how much stress are the parents under, too?

## Nadia

*One of the defining moments in our slow car crash of realisation that private prep school was entirely the wrong place for our girls to grow as human beings was the agony of prize day. In prep school terms, prize day is the ultimate experience in showboating. This was a day where certain children who had excelled over the year received a prize for outstanding academic achievements – but there were also prizes for things such as enthusiasm, team-playing and leadership.*

*Most of the parents we spoke to actually hated it and found it very stressful. In fact, more than a few slipped a little gin and tonic into their water bottles to get them through the hours of boring speeches and predictable winners! This was, as far as the school was concerned, a chance for them to show their markers of success.*

*There we all were, obedient parents, donning suits and cocktail dresses (FFS!), for this date in the calendar that was meant to be so very important. Each year we took our seats expectantly, only to slump down ever further in our chairs as we became just a little bit more jaundiced, feeling like it was little more than smoke and mirrors designed to make all us fee-paying parents feel like we were getting value for money.*

## Mark

*Most of the kids whose names were called out to receive awards for this or that academic achievement were the very same kids who were already in the top groups in their subjects, and who were all already 'dead certs' when it came to securing places at whatever their next elite and impressive school would be. Rather unimaginatively, the school would then award the same children with most of the non-academic awards. Call me old-fashioned, but if I wanted to motivate and mobilise the spirits of the non-academic kids, I would have at the very least garlanded them with the non-academic awards!*

*Meanwhile, patiently sitting there, our girls and all their friends who were in the lower streams had nothing to do but marvel at the academic high-achievers who would sometimes go up more than four times in one ceremony. In essence, those who already had an abundance of confidence* and were already seen as 'successful' were told again and again in front of the entire school and all the parents that they were indeed succeeding. And while all the others (including our girls) were not exactly told they were failing, their downturned heads as they left the huge posh hall told us everything we needed to know about what they were keeping to themselves.

●

Is money the marker of success – does it all return to money – whether it's the money we spend on our kids or the money our kids will potentially earn in life?

Maddie has talked about the fact that even the brightest kids in her first school feel that the school experience damaged them. If we are wondering why our children are encountering a generational crisis in their mental health (anxiety, depression, suicidal thoughts, addiction issues) could we perhaps be compassionate enough to maybe connect the dots? The one thing kids spend most of their time experiencing is school, in all its stressful manifestations. Isn't that a dot worth connecting? We believe there is an enormous disconnect between what education is meant to achieve and how it enters the minds and souls of children. The way we are mass-educating our children in no way caters for alternatives or difference. The aim of education is to systematise and make uniform young minds.

## Mark

*I was talking to my eldest daughter Issy only a couple of days ago about her circumstances in the post-lockdown 'new normal' after the coronavirus crisis. She is now twenty-six years old and sufficiently far away from graduating to have some perspective on the education she received and its varying merits in the outside world. She had been furloughed, and as a fine-art graduate had diversified her skills in the workplace in order to find a job. However, during lockdown, she found herself having the freedom to think and interrogate why the system of education she herself was a successful product of, in no way actually prepared her for the reality of being a working adult. She is in a place of disillusionment about the very structures of education that kept driving her on to the next juncture in order to facilitate the next chapter, and she's realised in lockdown that the entire kit and caboodle is something of a mirage. She feels like she's been sold a pup. Yes, she has a brilliant degree. Yes, she got all the grades she needed. But yes, the system has also left her rinsed out emotionally (struggling with anxiety herself) and broke (owing tens of thousands in student fees). For what reason? To take a job that isn't really the thing she wants to do, that doesn't pay enough money, within a system that places no value on creativity versus simply keeping the broader economy going. Issy's story is just one within a vast generation of febrile-minded youngsters disillusioned with the educative narrative they've been sold.*

*Once again, this isn't to say that the conventional system cannot work for many. Of course it can. You go into a prep school, you do your course, you go to law school and you become a lawyer. There are certain lines of work that have clear pathways, and certain kids who are happy to follow them. But what about the vast majority of youngsters who don't quite know what it is they want to do, because they've essentially been forced to tick so many boxes and jump through so many hoops in service of a system that has, as its main purpose, nothing more than its own smooth running? This is why university degrees are becoming increasingly devalued – as more and more people graduate, the specialness of having one slowly evaporates. More and more youngsters feel that the old-fashioned narrative of getting a degree to ensure a prosperous work life is defunct . . . and as technology and lifestyles change, they may well be right.*

●

But could the ultimate marker of success with our girls be the most curious outcome of all? For Maddie, success has been found in her love of the performing arts and her belief and desire to continue her education in this field. For Kiki, could the true success be her recent request to go to a particular type of school unlike any other in the country? A state school that *she* researched and decided could be right for *her*. A school where, yes you take the basic GCSEs (maths, English, science) but you can also take GCSEs in photography, art, fashion and set design. It's also a school that, funnily enough, quotes Sir Ken Robinson in its welcome pack!

We've both had to be brave. We've had to go against our initial fears. We've had to swim against our own internal currents as much as against those of society. We've doubted ourselves and each other. We've cried and we've laughed. But throughout it all, one of us has managed to steady the ship when the other has been just a little seasick and in danger of falling overboard.

As far as we're concerned, the entire point of the homeschooling project is to try and equip our kids with the self-confidence, self-belief and self-motivation to pursue their dreams and their passions in whatever way they feel is appropriate to them – even if that means actually deciding to go back into formal education!

As we sit here writing, both our girls have a passion for continually expanding their minds and their hearts. They love new experiences. They've discovered that learning doesn't have to be dull. They have seen connections between subjects that conventional learning would never choose to highlight. They are plugged into the real world, care passionately about the planet, and they recognise that hard work doesn't always have to translate into earning money.

But probably, the greatest marker of success is that neither of them believes learning has a finishing point.

They recognise that they can continue to self-educate and self-teach indefinitely.

It's not about learning to get past exam day.

It's about learning *every* day for the rest of their lives.

> *A self that goes on changing is a self that goes on living.*
>
> Virginia Woolf